William Atwood

The History, and Reasons, of the Dependency of Ireland Upon the Imperial Crown of the Kingdom of England

William Atwood

The History, and Reasons, of the Dependency of Ireland Upon the Imperial Crown of the Kingdom of England

ISBN/EAN: 9783337156046

Printed in Europe, USA, Canada, Australia, Japan

Cover: Foto ©ninafisch / pixelio.de

More available books at **www.hansebooks.com**

THE
History, and Reasons,
OF THE
Dependency of IRELAND
UPON THE
𝕴𝖒𝖕𝖊𝖗𝖎𝖆𝖑 𝕮𝖗𝖔𝖜𝖓
OF THE
Kingdom of ENGLAND.

Rectifying Mr. *Molineux*'s State of the Case of *Ireland*'s being bound by Acts of Parliament in *England*.

Actum erat de fœcundissimâ gente,
Si libera fuisset. Plin. Panegyr.

LONDON,
Printed for *Dan. Brown* at the Black Swan and Bible without *Temple-Bar*; and *Tho. Leigh* at the Peacock in *Fleetstreet*. 1698.

To the Honourable the Knights, Citizens, and Burgesses, in Parliament Assembled.

YOur House, and they (a) to whose Rights You succeed, having, for several Ages, been the Principal Support of the English Monarchy; the Enemies to so excellent a Constitution have thought it could never be more effectually undermined, than by the drawing your Rights into Question: and thus have many made in their deceitful Courts to Princes.

'Tis not for me to determine, whether Malice or Sycophantry have induced some to deny, your

(a) *Anciently there was but one House and sometimes one undivided Body sub dio. Thus one of K. Edgar's Charters An. 570. Non clam in angulo, sed sub Divo, palam evidentissimè scientibus totius regni mei Primatibus.*

a   being

Dedication.

being in any manner invested with that Authority, which they officiously ascribe to the Kings of this Realm, and their Council of Lords, or rather Privy Council; to the derogating from the Lords in Parliament, no less than from You.

I conceive it, allowable for me, to joyn the Men of this assurance with Dr. Brady, and other Advocates for Despotick Power: who have contended, that your first Presence, or Representation, in the National Council, began by Rebellion in the (d) 49. of H. 3. which being taken as proved, they conclude, that Kings may as well set you aside, as a

(d) Dr. Brady's Answer to Mr. Petty l. p. 1,2. To rescue these sacred things from groundless and designing interpretations: I follow his own Method, and do affirm, 1. That the Commons of England represented by Knights, Citizens, and Burgesses in Parliament were not introduced, nor were one of the three Estates in Parliament before the 49th of H. 3. 2. That before that time the body of the Commons of England, or Freemen as now understood or as we now frequently call them collectively taken, had not any share or vote in making of Laws for the government of the Kingdom, nor had any communication in Affairs of State, unless they were represented by the Tenants in Capite. Sub-

Dedication.

Subject may any obligation extorted by threats and duress.

And whoever has made any attempt towards the removing that Corner Stone for Tyranny, has been sure to incur the imputation of promoting Anarchy: as if your venerable Body did not in the least interpose between those two Extremes.

The fairest colour which the Men of Foreign Notions and Allegiance have, for their premises, is from King John's Charter, which as they imagine, has declared or establish'd the Tenents of the Crown in Chief, to be the only legal Members of the Common Council of the Kingdom; the far different sense of which Charter, I may well say 'twas my fortune to find and evince, upon my

first

Dedication.

(a) Vid. Jani Anglor. faciem nov. ed. An. 1680.
(b) Vid. Dr. Brady's Append. to his Compleat History cited in f.
(c) Dr. Brady's Introduct. f. 3, 6

(a) *first enquiry into the Nature of our Government; since the force of truth has obliged even* (b) *Dr. Brady to yield it up to me,* (c) *after all the hard Words which he had given me on that occasion.*

Speaking of Seditious Pieces design'd, *as* he says, to overturn the Government, and publish'd on purpose to usher in Anarchy and Confusion, (leaving a Blank for Mr. Petyt's Name, whom he sufficiently describes) these and other such stuff, says, he did mightily contribute to the Sedition and Rebellious Practices of a Great Man who laid violent Hands upon himself to prevent the Hand and Stroak of Justice. And like to this Piece are Jani Anglor. facies nova, Jus Anglorum ab antiquo, Reflections upon Antidotum Brit. &c. All written and timed to promote Sedition and in expectation of Rebellion and the destruction of the Establish'd Government.

(d) Jus Anglorum ab antiq.

Nor has he offered the least Shadow of Evidence against my List (d) from Domesday Book; shewing, that notwithstanding the supposed Conquest of this Land by W. 1. they who had not forfeited their Estates, enjoyed them upon or under Titles Priour to his Entrance; without relation to any Grant, or Confirmation from him.

Permit

Dedication.

Permit me to say, that the Researches in which this Controversy engaged me, have, in some measure, enabled me to assert your Authority, in the highest Instances of the exercise of *Power*; and to make out by *Deduction*, and numerous *Presidents*, what you have as 'twere by Intuition; *that* Ireland, *as 'tis* annexed to the Imperial Crown *of this Kingdom; is subjected to that Authority, which is, and must be absolute; and yet can never be grievous, because of your share in it.*

Tho the bold denial of this, has already receiv'd your just censure *of being* of dangerous Consequence to the Crown, and People of *England* : *Yet, if I may use the Allusion, I might observe, that 'tis not held improper to make* Comments *upon the* Sacred Text,

Votes, Lunæ, 27 Junii 1698.

Dedication.

Text, *to explain it to Vulgar Understandings: Which, I should hope, may plead in my Excuse, if not, Justification, while I am proving, that, as* you have *rightfully concurred with the* Lords, *in giving* Ireland *a King, by filling the* Vacant Throne; *and that* Glorious Preserver *of your Liberties has, with the* Advice *and* Consent *of the* States *of this his* Realm, *made Laws with a declared intention of binding* Ireland; *these Acts of* Sovereignty, *are not only agreeable to the Laws of Nature, and of Nations, but warranted by the* Ancient Constitution *of this* Monarchy.

The foundation of which, while I have been labouring to clear, from that Rubbish which would render it unstable; it has happened with me, as with those, who having exhausted

<small>Vid. Mat. Par. Addit. f. 281. De foris factu-râ regni per Johannem, & regni vacatio-ne per ejus-dem demissi-onem in manus Papæ.</small>

Dedication.

hausted themselves in working a rich Mine, are forced to leave the bright Oar to them that come after: And thus 'tis likely to be with those Collections which I have by me, concerning the Fundamental Constitution of this Government: by which I had flattered my self, that I must have contributed towards the Peace and Happiness of my Country, in shewing the admirable Harmony that there is between the constituent parts of this Empire; how strong and beautiful they are in their due order; How conspicuous that Degree of the Baronage, or Nobility of Engl. which you're present, has been in all the Ages of this Monarchy, in maintaining its Glory; what Persuasive Reasons both Prince and People have, to be satisfied with their several, and yet common

Dedication.

mon *Interests*; and how little they are to be thought *Friends* to either, who prompt them, as the Learned Grotius has it,

In partem non suam involare.

Whither I have been any way serviceable to the Publick, or can yet serve it, according to my Zeal; is submitted to the Collective Wisdom *of the Nation: The Judgment is with you; who, if you should not think this, or any of my former* labourous Effects of Idleness, *as the Poet calls the Writing of Books, worthy of your Protection, or Notice; I doubt not will extend your Pardon, to Endeavours consecrated to your use, By,*

Your Most Faithful and
Affectionate Humble Servant,

W. Atwood.

The History, and Reasons of the Dependency of Ireland, upon the Imperial Crown of the Kingdom of England, &c.

AS there's no need of staying for Publick Authority or Encouragement, to oppose an open Invasion upon the Rights of my Country; I cannot but think it my duty to make a stand, till better help come in, with Arms taken up on a sudden; and that the rather, since by a shew of Precedents, and popular Positions, some lovers of *English Liberties* are drawn in, to join with the *Invaders*: nor do I wonder, to find Sufferers under Arbitrary Reigns, easy to be misled, by a seeming * Advocate for *mankind*, who undertakes *the Cause of the whole Race of* Adam.

* *Mr. Molineux his Book, p. 3. I venture to expose my own weakness, rather than be wanting at this time to my Country, I might say indeed to mankind; for 'tis the Cause of the whole Race of Adam that I argue, &c.*

And yet to any man, who will be at the least pains to think of Consequences, 'twill be manifest, that the *Liberty* which the Gentleman, whom I oppose, contends for, *as the inherent Right of all mankind*, would be a total exemption from all Laws and Government, except such as *Adam* had a right to in the state of Nature: and, for want of knowing who has the title of Descent from him, would turn all Nations to such Commonwealths, wherein every *Paterfamiliâs* is an independent Soveraign. If men were to be considered in such a state, I will agree with him, That *on whatsoever ground any one Nation can challenge Liberty to themselves, on the same reason may the rest of* Adam's *Children expect it.*

But if this be taken with relation to the present Governments in the world; then, suppose this *Gentleman* hold a *Commonwealth* to be the freest state of *mankind*; to be uniform, he must believe, that no *Monarchies* ought to continue longer than the people should think fit: be-

Pag. 3.

because, according to his Maxim, the People of a Monarchy have the same right to *Liberty* that the others maintain: and, directly to the present question, no nation ought to have any dependence upon any other Nation. And, perhaps others will say, *neither ought they to have any protection.*

'Tis certain, that whether we consider the people of the same Nation, or the relation which one Nation has to another, their state or condition, must depend upon Constitutions and Agreements, express, or tacit. Indeed, what Constitutions and Agreements are binding, and for what time, will fall under the consideration of Reason, either of it self, or aided and assisted by Revelation. S. *Paul* having taught us, That *the Powers that are are ordained of God*; I should think that the *common practice of the world* (which this Gentleman admits to be against his Notions) is no small evidence of the right of Acquisitions made by one Nation upon, or over another: But if these could in right

Vid. Plin. Pan. Quàm nunc juvat, provincias omnes in fidem nostram deditionemq; venisse. Postquam contigit Princeps terrarum,&c.

Pag. 25.

be carried no further, than the * *damage sustained* by the injured Nation; the bounds of the Acquisitions would be very uncertain, and desultory.

> * *'Tis only damage sustain'd that gives title to another man's goods.*

That no true Principle opposes the Power, which *England* claims and exercises, over *Ireland*, might be shewn in a very narrow compass: Yet when many glittering Arguments are made use of, to support an unseasonable as well as groundless complaint; it may be requisite to give direct Answers to those things which may seem most plausible; and to lay such Foundations as may supersede the particular consideration of the rest: to which end I shall shew,

1. The nature of Mr. *Molineux* his Complaint.

2. The true Foundation and Nature of that *Right*, of which *England* is possessed, in relation to *Ireland*; and Mr. *Molineux*'s Mistakes, Omissions, and wrong Comparisons, and Inferences, concerning it.

3. That the Right which was at first acquired, is so far from being de-

departed from, that 'tis rather strengthened, and confirmed: and has been duly exercised, as the good of *England* has required, and in subordination to that: and, even in the greatest Instances now complained of.

4. That his Politicks, and seeming popular Notions, are wrong, and misapplied.

1*st.* Mr. *Molineux* would insinuate into his * Majesty's belief, in his *Dedication* to him, that some of late endeavour *to violate those Rights and Liberties,* which the *Irish,* or *English* there, *have enjoyed for above five hundred years:* And he plainly enough charges, both *Kings, Lords,* and *Commons* of *England,* and that acting *Parliamentarily,* not only with this endeavour, but with actual violations of that, which to him seems, the inherent Right *of all mankind.*

*Mr. Molineux his complaint against the Parliament of England. Vid. Dedication.

His Service to *his Country,* and to *all the Race of Adam,* he supposes to be call'd for, by *the present juncture of Affairs, when the business of* Ireland *is under the consideration of both Houses of the English Parliament:* Pag. 3.

that

that is, as his Margin explains it, the Case of the *Bishop of* Derry *in the House of Lords, and the prohibiting the exportation of the* Irish *Woollen Manufacture, in the House of Commons.*

P. 64, & 66. He complains, That Acts of Parliament in *England,* before the 10*th* of *H.* 4. and 29*th* of *H.* 6. had pretended to bind *Ireland,* without any confirmation there, tho they have not expresly claim'd this Right:

P. 68, 99. that there are modern Precedents of *English* Acts of Parliament pretending to bind *Ireland:* but these are *Innovations*; tho, of his own shewing, no more than was done before the

P. 105. 10*th* of *H.* 4. But he is *sorry to reflect*, that since the *late Revolution in these Kingdoms, when the Subjects of* England *have more strenuously than ever asserted their own Rights, and the Liberties of Parliaments, it has pleased them to bear harder on their poor Neighbours, than has ever yet been done in many Ages foregoing.*

P. 107. Nay but one Throne, tho two Kingdoms. The first attempt which this *Gentleman* complains of, since his Majesty's happy accession to the Throne

Throne of these Kingdoms, is an Act made, in great compassion, *for Relief of the Protestant Irish Clergy*: The next is one *prohibiting all* P. 108. *Trade and Commerce with* France; while *England* was engaged in an actual War, of which *Ireland* was a miserable Seat. Another is the Act *for the better security, and relief of their Majesties Protestant Subjects in* Ireland; *wherein* K. James's *Irish Parliament at* Dublin, *and all Acts and Attainders done by them are declared void*: And 'tis further provided, *That no Protestant shall suffer any Prejudice in his Estate, or Office, by reason of his absence out of* Ireland *since* December 25. 1685. *And that there should be a remittal of the King's Quit-Rent from* Decemb. 25. 1688. *to the end of the War.* And the last is, That *for abrogating the* P. 111. *Oath of Supremacy in* Ireland, *and appointing other Oaths.*

These are the *Acts of Parliament*, by the suppos'd submission to which, he will have it, that *the Rights of the People of* Ireland *have received the greatest weakening under his Majesty's jesty's Reign, and they are made of all his Majesty's Subjects the most unfortunate.*

Pag. 114.

These Acts are complained of, as Violations of the Rights of a *Kingdom* (*a*) *compleat and absolute in it self, without any* (*b*) *subordination to* England, *especially in relation to Parliaments:* That they are contrary to that (*c*) *amity* which should be maintained between *distinct Kingdoms,* or *the Children of one common Parent;* which *have distinct Rights, and Inheritances, absolutely within themselves:* and (*d*) *inconsistent with the Royalties, and Preeminence of a separate and distinct Kingdom.* (*e*) *Against the common Laws of* England, *which are in force both in* England *and* Ireland, *by the original Compact.* (*f*) *Against the Statute Laws both of* England *and* Ireland. (*g*) *Against several Charters of the Liberties granted to* Ireland. (*h*) *Against the King's Prerogative.* (*i*) *Against the practice of all former Ages.* (*k*) *Against several Resolutions of the learned Judges of former times.* Destructive of (*l*) *Property.* In-

(*a*) P. 128.
(*b*) P. 129, 133, 139.
(*c*) P. 147.
(*d*) P. 163.
(*e*) P. 154.
(*f*) P. 157.
(*g*) P. 161.
(*h*) P. 166.
(*i*) P. 168. Vid. e Cont. sup. p. 64, & 66.
(*k*) P. 170.
(*l*) Ibid.

of the Dependency of Ireland.

Introductive of *(m) the greatest confusion, and uncertainty imaginable.* And lastly, *(n) inconvenient for England,* being likely to *(o) make the Lords and People of* Ireland *think they are not well used, and may drive them into discontent.* And yet this Complaint must be thought very modest, because, *if the Great Council of* England *shall resolve the contrary,* he declares he shall *then believe himself to be in an Error, and with the lowest submission ask pardon for his assurance.*

(m) P. 171.
(n) Ibid.
(o) P. 172.
Pag. 3.

I cannot in the least question, but that *august and wise Assembly* will use that Method which he refers to for his Conviction: yet, since they are employed in Affairs of more immediate consequence, than the asserting and clearing the grounds of that Authority which they have long been possessed of; I shall think that I may do some service to my Country, in shewing,

2*ly.* The true Foundation of that Right, which *England* is possessed of, in relation to *Ireland*; and what are Mr. *Molineux's* principal Mistakes,

The true Foundation and Nature of the Right of England over Ireland.

Omis-

Omissions, and wrong Comparisons, and Inferences, concerning it. Here I hope to make it evident,

1. That he mistakes the Grounds for the submission of *Ireland* to H. 2. as well as the Nature of it; and omits material Passages which may illustrate that matter.

2. That if he had been as conversant in *Histories*, and *Records*, as he would be thought; he could never have had *assurance* enough to assert, *that England may be said much more properly to be conquer'd by* W. 1. *than* Ireland *by* H. 2.

Vid. p. 3.
p. 14.

3. That he is as much mistaken in his comparison between *Scotland* and *Ireland*; and that matter of his own shewing, or admission, might have convinced him of an *essential difference*.

Pag. 6.
Of the first annexation of the Land of Ireland *to the Crown of England.*

1. This *Gentleman* pretends to give the History of the *Expedition of the English into Ireland*; which he supposes to have been in the Reign of H. 2. and that all the Right which has been acquired by *England,* to have any Government, or Superiority, over that Nation, was

of the Dependency of Ireland.

was derived from within that King's Reign. Which manifests his having seen very little of our English Antiquities; and his not attending to what Irish Acts of Parliament might have taught him.

The Confessor's Law, under the Title *of the Rights and Appendages, or Dependencies, of the Crown of England*, expresly names *Ireland* as one, which it supposes to have been first annexed to the Crown of *England* by King *Arthur*. Accordingly, besides other Authorities which might be produced, a very Antient (*a*) Manuscript in Latin Verse in the *Cotton* Library, ascribed to a *Gildas*, who lived in the Year 860. speaking of several things done by that King in this British Kingdom, says;

Lambard's Archainomia, f. 148. de Jure & Appendiciis Coronæ Regni Britanniæ.

(*a*) Biblioth. Cot. sub effigie Julii.

B. 11.

His ita dispositis in regnum tendit Y-
(bernum.

" These things thus settled, he for
(Ireland goes.

Another (*b*) Manuscript in the *Cotton* Library, treating of the number

(*b*) Claudius. D. 2.

ber

ber of the Counties of *England*, and the *Countrys*, and *Iſlands*, which *of Right*, and *without doubt*, belong *to the Crown, and Dignity of the Kingdom of* Britain, and the ſeveral Laws or Cuſtoms, by which they were governed; among the places ſubject to the *Danelege*, mentions *Man*, the *Orcades*, (*c*) *Gurth*, and the *other Iſlands* of the *Weſtern Ocean*, about or in the way towards *Norway*, and *Danemark* : within which we may well think *Ireland* to have been meant, ſince the *Iſle of Man* is one of the Iſlands, there taken to be about, bordering upon, or in the Road to *Norway*, and *Denmark*.

Tho the *Confeſſor's* Law places the Foundation of the Right of the Crown of *England* to *Ireland*, in the acquiſition of King *Arthur*; it muſt be agreed, that this was ſo antiquated, and ſo many Changes had happened in the State of this Nation, between his time and King *Edgar's*, that he might well have no regard to any Right from King *Arthur*: And, however, might ſuppoſe himſelf to have been the firſt of

margin notes:
Na.
(c) Guernſey, *as* I take it.
Circa ἐν κύκλῳ.

of the Dependency of Ireland.

of the *Anglo-Saxon* Kings, who had *subjected Ireland, or the greatest part of it,* to *the Crown of England*; which that he did, we have the Testimony of his memorable Charter.

Ego Eadgarus Anglorum Basilius, omniumq; Regum insularum, quæ Britanniam circumjacent, cunctarumq; nationum quæ infra eam includuntur, Imperator, & Dominus; Gratias ago Deo Omnipotenti Regi meo, qui meum Imperium sic ampliavit, & exaltavit, super Regnum patrum meorum; qui, licet Monarchiam totius Angliæ adepti sunt, à tempore Ayelstani, qui, primus Regum Anglorum, Nationes quæ Britanniam incolunt sibi armis subegit: nullus	*I* Edgar, *King of the English, and Emperor and Lord of all the Kings of the Islands which lie about Britain, and of all Nations that are included within it, give Thanks to God Almighty my King, who hath so inlarged and exalted my Kingdom above the Kingdom of my Ancestors; who, altho they had gain'd the Monarchy of all England, from the time of King* Athelstan, *who was the first of the Kings of the English that brought under him by Arms the Nations which inhabit Britain: yet none of*	Rot. Cart. 5. E. 2 m. 12. n. 25. & 3 E. 3. m. 10. n. 23. Pro Priore & Conventu Wigorn. per inspeximus. An. 964. regni sui 6.

nullus tamen eorum ultra ejus fines, Imperium suum dilatare aggressus est. Mihi autem concessit propitia divinitas, cum Anglorum imperio, omnia Regna Insularum Oceani, cum suis ferocissimis Regulis, usque Norvegiam, maximamque partem Hiberniæ, cum suâ nobilissimâ civitate Dubliniâ, Anglorum regno subjacere. Quos etiam Armis meis imperiis colla subdere, Dei juvante gratiâ, coegi.	*of them attempted to stretch his Empire beyond its bounds. But the propitious Divinity has granted me, with the Empire of the English, to put under the Dominion of the English, all the Kingdoms of the Isles of the Ocean, with their fiercest little Kings, as far as Norway, and the greatest part of Ireland, with its most noble City Dublin: Even all those, by the help of God's Grace, I have compell'd to submit their Necks to my Commands.*

From this time 'twill be evident, to any who observe the stiles of our Kings, till *H.* II's time, that the Authority of *England* over *Ireland* was taken to be included under the stile of King of the English Saxons, of *Britain*, of the Island of *Albion*, or the like: not but that, for several Reigns

of the Dependency of Ireland.

Reigns before the time of *H.* II. Parliaments, in which the King's Charters pass'd, were often careful to have the stile more expressive of the Title to the Dominions out of *England.* For instances of both kinds :

Edgar, after the Charter above cited stiles himself,

Basileus dilectæ Insulæ Albionis, subditis nobis sceptris Regum Scottorum, Cumbrorumque ac Britonum, & omnium circumcirca Regionum.	*King of the Beloved Island of Albion, the Scepters of the Kings of the Scots, the Cumbers, and the Britons, being subject to us, and of all the Regions round about.*	Rot. Pat. 12. E. 2. m. 13. n. 42. Rot. Cart. 2. E. 3. m. 23. n. 78. An. 970. & Cart. Antiq. in Turr. Lond. B. n. 11.

In another ;

(*a*) Basileus Anglorum, & Imperator Regum Gentium.	*King of the English, and Emperor of the Kings of Nations.*	(*a*) Rot. Cart. 5. E. 2. m. 12. n. 25.

After this King *Ethelred* stiles himself sometimes ;

(*b*) Ego Adelred totius Albionis Monarchiam gubernans.	*I Athelred governing the Monarchy of all Albion.*	(*b*) Rot. Cart. 5. E. 3. m. 10. n. 17. per Prior & Convent. sanctæ Frischeswide. Oxon. An. 1084. regni 25.

Subscribes,
Rex Anglorum.   *King of the English.*

B   Some-

Sometimes,

(a) Rot. Cart. 5. E. 3. m. 32. n. 85. A. 979.

(a) Ego Athelred totius Britanniæ Basileus.

I Athelred *King of all* Britain.

Sometimes,

(b) Rot. Cart. 36. E. 3. m. 7. n. 3. A. 964.

(b) Ego Ethelred Britanniæ totius Anglorum Monarchus.

I Ethelred *Monarch of all the Britain of the Englisb.*

Sometimes,

(c) In Bib. Cot. An. 1001.

(c) Ego Ethelred totius Insulæ.

I Ethelred *King of the whole Island.*

Subscribes,

Rex & Rector Angulsexna.

King and Ruler of the Anglo-Saxons.

That *Ireland* and other Kingdoms and Dominions, were included within this ftile, will appear by other Charters of the fame King. Thus he ftiles himself,

(d) Monaſt. 1. vol. f. 94. à. A. 983.

(d) Totius Anglorum Gentis Basileos, cæterarumque Nationum in circuitu perfiftentium, primatum gerens.

King of all the Engliſh Nation, and having the Supremacy over the other Nations living round about.

At

of the Dependency of Ireland.

At another time he stiles himself;

(*a*) Ego Ethelred Rex Anglorum, aliarumque gentium in circuitu persistentium.

I Ethelred *King of the English, and other Nations living round about.*

(*a*) Rot. Cart. 5. E. 3. m. 32. n. 85. pars unica. A. 987.

And the same stile (*b*) he uses in the Year 1001. tho, as appears above, in another Charter of the same Year, he stiles himself only *King of the whole Island*. And in another, (*c*) at the beginning of his Reign, only *King of the English*.

(*b*) Hist. Elyens. in Bib. Cotton.

(*c*) Vid. Rot. Cart. 2. R. 2. m. 13. n. 5. Bib. Cot. sub. effig. Claudii c. 9. Hist. Eccles. Abind. Cart. Antiq. B. n. 4. K. n. 22.

W. I. generally stiles himself no more than *King of the English*, or *King of the English, and Duke of Normandy*. Yet, as one of his Charters has it, he was (*d*) *the most powerful of all the Kings of that time, ruling the greatest Empire of England*. That other Nations were then held to be Dependencies upon the Kingdom of *England*, appears by a Charter of his in the 15*th* of his Reign, which begins;

(*d*) Cartæ Antiquæ in Turri Lond. D. n. 12. Cœnob. de Salebia.

(*e*) Ego Gulielmus Deo disponente rex Anglorum, cæterarumque gentium cir-

I William *by God's Disposal King of the English, and Ruler of the rest of the Nations round*

(*e*) Cart. Antiq. Q. n. 2. An. 1081.

circumquaq; persi- round about, and
stentium Rector, & Duke of Norman-
Dux Normannorū. dy.

After his time his Successors, till *H.* 2. left the Dependencies of *England* out of their Stile, adding only other Dominions, which they had as distinct and independent.

Thus *H.* 1. to mention no other, stiles himself *King* of the *English*, and *Duke* of *Normandy*; but before the death of his Brother *Robert*, only * *King* of the *English*.

* Bib. Cot. sub Effigie Claudii 9 Regist. Abind. *dehund. de Hormmere.*

Of the Superiority and Authority of the Church of England over the Church of Ireland.

Not here to bring other Evidences, of the continuance of the Superiority over *Ireland*; to turn † Mr. *Molineux* his Argument upon him, if I shew the *Church* of *Ireland* to have been then dependent upon, or under the *Church* of *England*, he must not deny but the State was too.

Archbishop *Parker*, who must be allowed to have seen and understood the Evidences of the Rights of the *See* of *Canterbury*, and is agreed to be

* *Parker's Antiq. Brit.* Et quiq; Nobiles cum Clero.

---

† P. 129. *If our Church be free and absolute within it self, our State must be so too.*

of the Dependency of Ireland.

be a faithful *Collector*, speaking of the time of *H.* 1. shews, that upon the vacancy of the Bishoprick of *Waterford, Murchertach* King of *Ireland,* with *the Bishops, all the Nobility,* and the *Clergy,* and *People* of the Island, sent to *Anselm* Archbishop of *Canterbury,* desiring

Quatenus ipse, primatûs quem super eos gerebat potestate, & quâ fungebatur Apostolicâ fretus Authoritate, sanctæ Christianitati, ac necessariæ plebium utilitati eis subveniret.	*That by the Power of the* Supremacy *which he had over them, and the Apostolical Authority which he enjoyed, he would be aiding to holy Christianity, and the necessities of the people.*

* At their *request,* he upon the death of the Bishop of *Dublin,* consecrated one *Malchus,* whose Bishoprick † Pope *Eugenius* raised into an *Arbishoprick:* But notwithstanding the Popes, *Eugenius* and *Adrian,* had constituted Archbishops there; yet they all acknowledged ‖ the *Supremacy* of the See of *Canterbury in all things.*

* Petitioni eorum Annuit.

† Fo. 23. Ann. 1151.

Ibid.

‖ Ib. F. 23. Nihilominus Cant. Primatem in omnibus agnoscunt.

B 3 And

And after Archbishop *Parker* had enumerated 33 *Bishopricks* in *Ireland*, he adds,

<small>* Antiq. Brit.] sup.</small>

* Hi omnes 33 Episcopatus, usitato & antiquissimo regni jure, ac instituto, Cantuar. sedi ut Metropoli parent.

All these 33 Bishopricks, by the accustomed and most antient Right and Constitution of the Kingdom, obey the See of Canterbury as the Metropolis.

If it were doubtful whether he meant that this *Right* was, by the antient *Constitution* of the Kingdom of *England*, the former Authorities make it evident that it was. However I shall confirm them with two more.

<small>Inter decem script. Gerv. Dorob. Actus Pontif. Cant. F.1633. Ann. 605.</small>

Gervace of *Canterbury*, who lived in the time of *H.* 2. speaking of *Lawrence* Archbishop of *Canterbury*, who succeeded the reputed *English* Apostle *Austin*, says,

<small>Nec non & Scothorū qui Hiberniam insulam Britanniæ proximam incolunt, pastoralem impendere sollicitudinem curabat.</small>

He not only took care of the *new Church* gathered out of the *English*,

but

of the Dependency of Ireland.

but of the *old British Inhabitants*; and also took care of his *pastoral Charge over the Scots,* who inhabit *Ireland,* an Island very near *Britain.*

Bromton, an Author who is cited by Mr. *Molineux,* mentioning the Dispute about *Superiority,* in the *Great Council,* or *Parliament* at *Winchester,* in the beginning of the Reign of *W.* 1. between *Lanfranc* Archbishop of *Canterbury,* and the then Archbishop of *York,* says *,

Brompton, F. 970, 971. de An. 1071.

* *Not that the whole History need have been read in the Council, but the chief Passages produced by them who had read it.*

Ubi Historia Bedæ perlectâ, monstratum est, à tempore primi Augustini usque ad ultima Bedæ tempora, quod circiter centum quadraginta annos erat, Cantuar. Arch. primatum super totam Britannicæ Insulam, & Hiberniæ gessisse.	*Where the History of* Bede *having been read,* 'twas shewn *that from* Austin's *first coming to the end of* Bede, *which was about* 140 *years, the Archbishop of* Canterbury *held the Primacy over the whole Island of* Britain, *and of* Ireland.

Thus I think 'tis past dispute, that a superiority of Government, both

The History and Reasons

both in *Church* and *State*, was vested with the *English*, and by consequence in the Crown of *England* as the *Head*, from the *6th* of King *Edgar* at the lateſt, to the year 1151. when the Juriſdiction of *Anſelm* Archbiſhop of *Canterbury* was ſubmitted to by the *Iriſh*, as the antient and undoubted Right of that See.

Nor can it be imagined, without ſome account of the Circumſtances, that the Superiority and Authority of *England* ſhould have been loſt in leſs than 22 years, when Mr. *M.* ſuppoſes the Pretenſions of *England* to have had their firſt ground.

<small>P.8. An. 1172.</small>

<small>P. 6, 7, 8. Of H.2d's landing in Ireland.</small>

He will have *H.* 2. his landing in *Ireland*, to have been occaſioned only by a fortunate Expedition thither by ſome of his Subjects a little before; in aſſiſtance of ſome of the Princes, or Kings of *Ireland*, who had been oppreſs'd by a too powerful Neighbour; and would inſinuate as if the *Deliverers* were only entituled to be paid for the aſſiſtance which they gave: and he is ſo bountiful,

tiful, as to *allow that* England *ought* P. 144. *to be repaid all their Expences in suppressing the late Rebellion.*

But, as *England* has suppreſt that Rebellion againſt the *Engliſh Crown,* it appears by what has been above cited, that the diſputes between the Kings of *Ireland* only gave *H.* 2. opportunity, and encouragement, to aſſert the Authority of the *Engliſh Nation,* and to reſtore to the Crown the poſſeſſion of the City of *Dublin,* and ſo much of the *Engliſh Pale* as could then be gained, with ſuch addition as they could make in a juſt War, to ſecure thoſe Bounds which had been invaded, and uſurped upon by a barbarous Enemy.

In this *H.* 2. was not to be blamed, for that Ambition which has carried Princes to make *Conqueſts*; ſince his Expedition was no more than he was obliged to as *King* of *England*: For as the *Confeſſor*'s Law has it, *The juſtification of H. 2d's Expedition.*

Debet

Lambard's Archaionómia, F. 138. De Regis Officio, &c.

Debet vero de jure Rex omnes terras, & honores, omnes dignitates, & jura, & libertates coronæ regni hujus, in integrum, cum omni integritate, & sine diminutione, observare, & defendere; dispersa, & dilapidata, & omissa, regni jura, in pristinum statum & debitum, viribus omnibus revocare.	But the *King* ought of right *to keep and defend all the Lands, and Honours, all Dignities, & Rights, and Liberties, of the Crown of this Kingdom, with all integrity, and without diminution: with all his might, to bring back to the antient and due state, the dispersed, dilapidated, and lost Rights of the Kingdom.*

This was not only incumbent upon the Prince, but upon the People also, who were *sworn Brethren to defend the Kingdom* against Strangers, and against Enemies, together with their Lord and King; and *with him,* to keep *his Lands,* and *Honours,* with all Fidelity.

Vid. Leges St. Edw. Tit. Greve.

Accordingly, when the Pope cited *E.* 1. to answer judicially before him, concerning his Right over *Scotland,* the *Parliament* say,

" The

of the Dependency of Ireland.

" The Premises would manifest- *Ryley's* Placita Parl. 29 E. 1.
" ly turn to the *disherison of the*
" *Right of the Crown of the King-*
" *dom of* England, *and of the Royal*
" *Dignity,* and *notorious subversion*
" *of the state of the said Kingdom :*
" And also to the prejudice of *the*
" *Liberties,* the *Customs,* and *Laws*
" *of our Ancestors.* To the obser-
" vation of which we *are bound,*
" *by virtue of the Oath we have tak-*
" *en*; and *which we will maintain*
" *with all our Power, and, by God's*
" *assistance, will defend, with all our*
" *might.* Nor *also do we, or can we,*
" *as indeed we may not, suffer our*
" Lord the *King, even tho he would,*
" to do, *or in any wise attempt the*
" *Premises,* &c.

Here's a ground to justify *H.* 2. and the *People* of *England* at that time; which *this Gentleman* never thought of.

And *Giraldus Cambrensis,* an Author received by him, and an *Irish* Vid. Inf. Parliament, has shewn another, from the nature of the *Irish,* the necessity of their Reformation, and that Authority

thority which the generality of Christians in those dark Ages placed in the Pope.

As to the Character of the People, after *Girald* had condemned their Clergy, for not doing their duty among them, he says,

Anglia sacra, Giraldus Cambrensis de rebus a se gestis, Pars 2. c. 14.

Ut enim de perjuriis eorum, & proditionibus, de furtis, & latrociniis, quibus totus hic populus prope modum, immo præter modum, indulget; de vitiis variis & immunditiis nimis onormibus, quas topographia declarat, ex toto non emittamus; Gens hæc Gens spurcissima, Gens vitiis involutissima, Gens omnium Gentium in fidei rudimentis incultissima.

For not wholly to omit speaking of their Perjuries *and* Treasons, *of the Thefts and Robberies which this whole people in some measure, rather without measure, indulges; of their various vices and uncleannesses too enormous, which our* Topography *declares;* This Nation is a Nation most vile, a Nation the most drown'd in Vices, a Nation of all Nations the most ignorant in the Rudiments of Religion.

This being the nature of the People at that time, there might seem, if

of the Dependency of Ireland.

if there had been no prior Title, to have been as much a right of *occupancy*, as any Nation has had by the first possessing the Lands of Savages: but if the right of civilizing the barbarous part of Mankind was not sufficient, that Power which the then general consent of Nations had placed in the Pope, joined with the other, made a Title, which none but the Barbarians then disputed. This *H. 2.* had amply and formally.

Giraldus Cambrensis not only informs us, that the *Pope* gave *H. 2.* licence to subdue the *Irish*, but exhibits the *Bull* at large, which, reciting the King's Intention of entring the *Island* of *Ireland*,

^{Angl. sac. sup. pars 2. F. 485. speaking of King John, Pater ipsius intrandi Hiberniam, sibiq; subjugandi, ab ecclesia Romana licentiam impetravit.}

| Ad subdendum populum illum legibus, & vitiorum plantaria inde extirpanda, & de singulis domibus annuam unius denarii B. Petro velle solvere pensionem, & jura | To subdue that people to Laws, and extirpate the plantations of Vices from thence; and that he will pay to St. Peter the annual Pension of a Penny out of every House, and preserve |

The History and Reasons

jura Ecclesiarum terræ illius illibata & integra confervare;	*ferve the Rights of the Churches of that Land unprejudiced and entire;*

Declares the Pope's approbation of that King's attempting that Island, *for enlarging the bounds of the Church, for restraining the course of Vices, for correcting their Manners, and sowing Virtues, for the encrease of the Christian Religion.*

Pro dilatandis Ecclesiæ terminis, &c.

And this Pope desires the King's purpose may take effect, for *the Honour of God, and Salvation of that Land*; and that the People of that *Land* should receive him honourably, and reverence him *as their Lord.*

Jure nimirum e contrario illibato & integro permanente, & salva B. Petro & S. R. E. de singulis domibus unius denarii pensione.	*The Right however remaining unprejudiced and entire, and saving to St. Peter, and the holy Church of Rome, the pension of a Penny out of every House.*

of the Dependency of Ireland.

The Right of the Church was hereby reserv'd unprejudiced: the Recital seems to make it to relate to the particular Churches; and this Mr. *Molineux*, if he please, may take to amount to such a Freedom, as exempted them from the Jurisdiction of the Pope, as well as of the See of *Canterbury*: but he may easily observe that the Superiority of both is fully reserved, and implied under *jure illibato & integro permanente*.

V. p. 129. Holy Church shall be free, &c. If our Church be free and absolute within itself, our State must be so likewise.

It thus appearing, that this Gentleman had not attended to the true grounds of *H. 2d's* Attempt upon *Ireland*, I shall consider what Submission the Irish made to him, and in what sense he and his Parliament took it. 'Tis evident beyond contradiction, that they did not submit to him as to a King, whom they chose to govern according to their own Laws, but as one that imposed, and was to impose Laws upon them: Of this Mr. *Molineux* seems so much aware, that where he speaks of the submitting to *H.* 2. he only mentions the general terms of receiving *P. 10, & 11.*
him

him for *King and Lord* of *Ireland*, and swearing Allegiance to him and his Heirs, or the like: but the swearing to the Laws of *England* he places among the *Concessions*; as if they were no otherwise subject to them than the People of *England*.

P. 28.

Of the Submission of the Irish to H. 2.

'Tis to be observed, for proof that the Submission was truly voluntary, and that there was such a Consent as is essential to the making Laws to bind Posterity; that upon *H.* 2's landing at *Waterford*, several of the Irish Kings, and almost all the Nobility of *Ireland* flock'd in to him; that the Archbishops, Bishops, and Abbats of all *Ireland* receiv'd him for *King and Lord* of *Ireland*, and swore to him and his Heirs, binding themselves by their Charters to perpetual Allegiance; and that after their example, and in like manner, the Kings and Princes there present receiv'd him for Lord and King of *Ireland*.

V. p. 10. Cited by him.

Upon which I need not observe the known difference taken in *Pliny*, and other good Authors, between *Dominus* and *Princeps*; since after

of the Dependency of Ireland.　33

this the King held a Council at *Lismore*, cited by this Gentleman in a wrong place.

P. 28.

| Ubi leges Angliæ sunt ab omnibus gratanter receptæ & juratoriâ cautione confirmatæ. | *Where the Laws of* England *are thankfully received of all, and confirm'd by a juratory Caution.* |

And for a farther Security, the King possest himself of several Cities and Castles, which he put into safe hands; but of this Mr. *M.* takes no notice.

Mat. Par. ib. Urbes & Castella quæ Rex in sua receperat, sub fideli custodia deputavit.

As a cotemporary Exposition is ever of greatest Authority, let's see whether the meaning of this was, that *Ireland* was to be governd by Parliaments of its own, as *free and independent* as *England*; or that it should be governed by the Laws *made*, and *to be made*, by *England*.

Mr. *Molineux* confesses, that *H.* II. within five years after his Return from *Ireland* created his younger Son *John* King of *Ireland*, at a Parliament held at *Oxford*: he might have learn'd from the same Authority,

P. 29.

C

rity, that in that Parliament he not only disposed of several petty Kingdoms there, to hold of him and *John* his Son, but *Hoveden* has these words, which comprehend Lands as well as Governments.

Hoveden. f. 323.

F. 324.

| Postquam autem Dominus Rex apud Oxenford, in prædicto modo, terras Hiberniæ & earum servitia divisisset; fecit omnes quibus earundem custodias commiserat, homines suos & Johannis filii sui devenire. | But after the Lord the King had at Oxford, *in manner aforesaid, divided the Lands of* Ireland *and their Services; he caused all those, to whom he had committed the Custody of them, to do homage to him and his Son* John, *& to swear Allegiance and Fidelity to them.* |

Int. Decem script. Bromton de eod. An.

Bromton says;

| Apud Oxoniam idem Rex Angliæ Johannem filium suum, coram Episc. & regni sui Princip. Regem Hiberniæ constituit. Et postea fecit quosdam familiares suos sibi & Johanni filio suo ligantias, fidelitates & | *At* Oxford *the said King constituted his Son* John *King of* Ireland, *before the Bishops and Princes of his Kingdom. And afterwards he made some of his Courtiers to do and swear Allegiance, Fidelity, and Homage to himself and* |

of the Dependency of Ireland.

& homagia, contra omnes homines, facere & jurare. Quibus terras Hiberniæ dedit & distribuit in hunc modum, &c.

and his Son John, *against all men: To whom he gave and distributed the Lands of* Ireland *in this manner*, &c.

If what the King did in a Parliament was a Parliamentary Act, here was an Act of the English Parliament, which, by Mr. *Molineux*'s Confession, *impos'd a King upon Ireland*, to whom they had not sworn any otherwise than as they swore to submit to the English Laws: and he should have observed, that herein, according to his own inference, of the making *Ireland* a separate Kingdom, the English Parliament undertook to discharge the Oath which the Irish had taken to be true to *H*. 2. and his Heirs; and sutably to the Legislative Authority over *Ireland* in this Particular, the same Parliament at *Oxford* disposed of and distributed the Lands of *Ireland*, without expecting any Ratification from thence.

Here's a Parliamentary and cotemporary

Vid. Inf. *In truth he was but Viceroy.*

V. p. 10. Jurantes ei & hæredibus suis

temporary Expofition, of what this Gentleman calls the *Original Compact* between *England* and *Ireland*.

P. 154.

I muſt agree, tho he has not obſerv'd it, that notwithſtanding H. II's Acquiſition in *Ireland*, an Iriſh Native had quiet poſſeſſion of a Kingdom which he ſeem'd to claim as chief King over the Iriſh. This was *Roderic* King of *Connaught*, who upon paying his Tribute, and performing his appointed Service, was, (*a*) according to *Hoveden*, to hold his Land as he held it before H. II. enter'd *Ireland*: which could not be true in a ſtrict ſenſe, unleſs he were dependent upon the Crown of *England* before; and however, this was a Grant after a more abſolute Acquiſition: and (*b*) three years after, *Girald* holds, as do the Iriſh Statutes, that he had (*c*) conquer'd the whole Land of *Ireland*.

(*a*) Hoveden. f. 312. Sicut tenuit antequam dominus Rex intravit Hib.
(*b*) An. 1175.
(*c*) Gir. Cambr. expug. Hib. c. 34. de An. 1177. Anno primo quo illuſtriſſimus Anglor. R. & Hib. triumphator, ipſam inſulam acquiſivit.
(*d*) Benedict. Abbas, p. 69. cited in Dr. Bradey's Append. f. 39.

(*d*) Abbat *Benedict*, an Author of that time, to be ſeen in the *Cotton* Library, ſpeaking of H. II. ſays,

Concedit Roderico ligio ſuo Regi Conautæ, quamdiu ei fide-

He grants to Roderic *his Leige-man*, *King of* Connaught, that

of the Dependency of Ireland. 37

fideliter serviet, ut sit Rex sub eo, paratus ad servitium suum: salvo in omnibus jure & honore Domini Regis Angliæ, & suo.	that as long as he faithfully served him, he should be a King under him, ready for his Service: saving in all things the Right and Honour of the Lord the King of England, and his.

As it appears by Record, by the 7th of King *John*, the King of *Connaught* had two thirds duly taken from him, for not performing his Service; or else he never had more than a third of that Kingdom granted; for then he acknowledged that he held a 3d part in the name of a Barony, and for the other two thirds proffers the King, *Rot. Clauf. 7. Jo. m. 5.* *Nomine Baroniæ.*

Duos Cantredos, cum Nativis eorundem Cantredorum, de prædictis duabus partibus, ad firmandum in eis, vel faciendum inde voluntatem suam.	*Two Cantreds, with the Natives of those Cantreds, to let 'em to farm, or to do with them what he pleased.*

Thus I take it, his Kingdom was as much dependent upon the Crown

C 3 of

of *England*, as any Barony in *Ireland*, or *England*, and as subject to Forfeiture.

<small>Davis Rep. f. 38.</small>

And 'tis probable, that this King was the head of the *O Conoghors* of *Connaught*, who are, 3 *E*. 2. admitted to be entituled to the English Law.

But tho the Law of *England* was not current beyond the English Pale, or those *Cantreds* and Divisions of *Irish*, who continued under Obedience to the English; yet the Crown of *England* has, from very antient times, not only laid claim to the Lordship over the whole Land of *Ireland*, but their Parliaments have recognized this Right more than once.

<small>Of the Antiquity of the Right of the Crown of England to the Land of Ireland, recognized by Parliaments there. Stat. 11 Eliz. Sef. 3. c. 1. f. 273.</small>

Mr. *M*. if he had pleased, might have found, that Acts of Parliament made in *Ireland* lay a much earlier Foundation of the Right of the Crown of *England* to the Land of *Ireland*, even than our Confessor's Law does. A Statute made in *Ireland*, 1 *Eliz*. among *sundry Titles*, which the antient Chronicles in the Latin, English and Irish Tongues, alledge for the Kings of England to

the

the Land of Ireland, derives one from *Gormond* Son of *Belin*, King of *Great Britain*.

This King our Hiſtorians call *Gurgunſtus*, and is ſaid to have reign'd in *Great Britain* 375 years before the *Chriſtian Æra*. *Grafton*, agreeing with the Iriſh Statute, tells us, that in his return from *Denmark*, he met with a Fleet of *Spaniards*, which were ſeeking for Habitations, to whom the King granted the Iſle of *Ireland* to inhabit, and *to hold of him as their Sovereign Lord*. Grafton de an. ante Chriſtum 375. De eod. an.

The Statute made in *Ireland*, 13 *C.* 2. recognizing his Title, has theſe words; "Recognitions of this "nature may ſeem unneceſſary "where your Majeſty's Title to "this your Realm is ſo clear, as "that it is avowed in *ſundry Acts* "*of Parliament heretofore made* "*within this Kingdom, in the times* "*of your Majeſty's Royal Progenitors* "of famous memory: and SO ANTIENT, AS IT IS DEDUCED "NOT ONLY FROM THE "DAYS OF KING *H.* 2. your "Majeſty's Royal Anceſtor, BUT *Iriſh Stat.* f. 493.

"FROM TIMES FAR MORE ANTIENT, AS BY SUNDRY AUTHENTICK EVIDENCES MENTIONED IN THE SAID ACTS, AND RECORDS OF THIS YOUR MAJESTY'S KINGDOM, MAY EVIDENTLY APPEAR.

Since Mr. *Molineux* allows Acts of Parliament made in *Ireland*, to have full Authority; I hope he will confess, that he has given a very imperfect and undue account how *Ireland* became a Kingdom annexed to the Crown of *England*; and thus, not here to observe that he need not have gone so far back to shew how it first became a Kingdom, I think I have made it evident, that he has fail'd in his first Undertaking.

P. 4.

Of the comparison between W. 1. and H. 2. and of the stile and notion of Conquest.

Davis's Rep. f. 41. Case de Tanistry.

2. 'Twill be as evident, that he is no less injurious to the Right of the English Nation, than unhappy in the comparison, where he maintains, that England *may be said much more properly to be conquer'd by* W. 1. *than* Ireland *by* H. 2. tho in this he has the Authority of Sir *John Davis*. I will agree, that the word *Conquest* was in the times both of *W.* 1. and
H. 2.

of the Dependency of Ireland.

H. 2. of a very innocent signification; for which he rightly cites Sir *Henry Spelman*, and might have observed a much greater and antienter Authority, in a Record of the time of King *John*, referr'd to by (*a*) Mr. *Petyt*: wherein a younger Brother, in a Suit between him and his elder Brother about Title to Land, pleads, that his Father had it *de Conquestu suo*, and gave it him; according to the distinction in *Glanvil*, who wrote in the time of *H.* 2. between (*b*) *Questus*, the same with *Conquestus*, and *Hæreditas*. 'Tis certain the word *Conquestus* did not in that age imply any thing of that Power, which a Prince or State might acquire, by Force or Terror of Arms, over another Prince or State; and therefore I shall make no use of his Admission, that *H.* 2. took *Conquestor Hiberniæ* into his stile, contrary to the Authority of (*c*) Mr. *Selden*, cited in his Margin, and to which I cannot but subscribe. In truth, tho (*d*) *H.* 2. was stiled Lord of Ireland, I am very well assured none can be found where he is stiled

(♥) 12, & 13.

(*a*) Vid. *Mr. Petyt's Pref. to the Rights of the Kingdom.* Mic. 2. Jo. *The same transcribed more at large in* Hales's *Collect. in Bib.* Hospitii Lincoln.

(*b*) Glanvil. de legibus, lib. 7. c. 1. Vid. ib. aut habet hæreditatem tantum, aut questum tantum.

(*c*) P. 14.
(*d*) Vid. Pref. *to* Davis's *Rep. The first after the Norman Conquest that was stiled* Lord of Ireland.

styled *Conqueſtor*. Yet *Girald*, an Author of that time, calls him, *Triumphator Hiberniæ*, which is tantamount to Conqueror. But since *Conqueſtor*, when firſt uſed, ſignified no more than one who came to a Right which he claimed not by *hereditary Deſcent* (according to which *W*. 1. acknowledged, that he was *made* or *created* King of the Engliſh by hereditary *Right*, that is, as has elſewhere been ſhewn, and may be more at large, was duly let in to the Inheritance of the Crown) however the word *Conqueſtor* has been in following ages applied both to *W*. 1. and to *H*. 2. Let's conſider a little,

1. Whether the Engliſh Nation ever ſubmitted to *W*. 1. as a Conqueror, in a ſenſe of larger ſignification than 'twas antiently uſed.

2. Whether the Iriſh Nation ſubmitted to *H*. 2. or to any other of our Kings, more abſolutely than the Engliſh did to *W*. 1.

1. Mr. *Molineux* agrees, that *E*. 3. was the firſt that us'd the *Æra* of *poſt Conqueſtum*; which indeed was no more than to diſtinguiſh the *Edwards*

Margin notes:
Girald. Camb. Hibern. expugnat.

Vid. Reflections upon a treaſonable Opinion againſt ſigning the voluntary Aſſociation.

p. 14.

pendency of Ireland.   43

he time of *W.* 1. from
wards which reign'd in
ore that time : but no
 know of, has yet
iat *W.* 1. ever assumed
Conqueror; and I dare
Author of that time,
n Manuscript, ascribes
 must own in some of
 he says, he *gain'd the
the Sword, having sub-
and his Accomplices:*
hat *Puffendorf's* Asser-   Puff. de Jure
eniable; that *after a*   Gentium.
rcome in a just War, till VII. 7. 3.
onsent, the State of War
nd there is no Obligation
d so no Dominion*; W.* 1.
 to civilize and subdue
to Laws, but to turn
n Usurper upon the
e People, upon whom
posed himself without
&ction, notwithstanding
l antient Authors have
And, 2*dly.* An Usurper
ight which *W.* 1. had,
d a formal Election, he
elected Successor in the
life

life time of the Confessor: which I may hereafter shew, with all the Circumstances, but shall at present refer only to three Authorities out of many.

William of *Poictiers*, an Author who lived in the very time, informs us, that the Confessor sent an Embassy into *Normandy*, *suorum assensu*, by the *assent of his People*; to assure him of the Succession.

<small>Pictav. gesta W. Ducis Norm. & Regis Anglor. f. 181.</small>

And *Ordericus Vitalis* has these words.

<small>Ord. Vital. f. 492.</small>

| Edwardus nimirum propinquo suo W. D. N. primo per Rodbertum Cant. summum Pontificem, postea per eundem Heraldum, integram Anglici regni mandaverat concessionem: ipsumque, concedentibus Anglis, fecerat totius juris sui hæredem. | Edward *sent an Embassy to* William *Duke of* Normandy, *first by* Robert *Archbishop of* Canterbury, *afterwards by* Harold *himself*, *acquainting him with the entire Grant of the Kingdom of* England: *and had made him Heir of all his Right*, with the Consent of the English. |

Which shews in what sense *Ingulph*, who was Secretary to *W.* 1. is to be understood, when he says, That

of the Dependency of Ireland.

Eum sibi succede-	That *the* Confes-
re in regnum voce	sor, *with a stable*
stabili sancivit.	*Voice ordained, or*
	appointed him to suc-
	ceed him in his King-
	dom.

'Tis not to be questioned, but *Ingulph* who was an *Anglo-saxon*, and well knew that a King could not dispose of the English Crown, without the consent of the *States of the Realm*; would be understood by this, that the *Confessor's voice*, or *nomination*, had a *Parliamentary Sanction*; when one of the *Norman* writers looks upon *Harold* as a * *madman*, for not staying to see what a *publick Election* should determine.

That *W.* 1. came only to turn out an Usurper, is not all: but having done this with a great force, the People of *England* would not receive him for King upon his Victory, till they had treated and agreed with him in a † *Convention* at *Berkhamstead*; where, as Authors concur, *fœdus pepigit*, "he struck a "League with them; and was not only obliged to maintain the *English*

* Non expectabat vesanus Anglus quid publica electio statueret. Pictav. ut memini, vel Ordir. Vital.

† Flor. Wig. Fidelitat. juraverunt, quibus & ipse fœdus pepigit. S. Dunelm. F. 195. Hoveden. F. 258. Rad. de Diceto Col. 480. Bromton Col. 958.

lish Laws, in virtue of a *mutual Contract*: but part of the *Contract* with the ‖ *Prelats*, and the *Nobility of the Kingdom*, was, That he should be *crown'd as the manner of the English Government requires*. From those Authors who give the heads of his Oath, administred by *Aldred* Archbishop of *York*, 'tis plain, that he was crown'd according to the *standing Ritual* in use from the Coronation of King *Ethelred*, and continued to the Reign of *H*. 1. without any material alteration: And *Authors*, as well as the *Ritual*, shew, that the people were solemnly ask'd, *whether they would have him to reign over them?* to which they exprest their *consent*, in such terms as implied a * *Grant*.

‖ Ordir. Vital. F. 503.

Bib. Cotton. sub Effigie Claudii, A. 3.

* Bib. Cot. sup. Volumus & concedimus.

But the *Coronation Oath* being only in general terms; that King was obliged, once at least, if not oftner, to swear expresly, that they should enjoy the Benefit of the *Confessor*'s Laws; that Digest of so much of the common Law of *England*, as was in his time thought necessary to be reduced to writing; to which some

Vid. Selden. Dissert. ad Fletam de confirmatione, 4º Regni sui E-kal. vid. etiam Mat. Par. Addit. de Fretherico Ab. Sancti Albani, extorquente cautionem juratoriam.

of the Dependency of Ireland.

some additions were made by that King *in Parliament, for the benefit of the English.*

That there was nothing like this, in the submission of the people of *Ireland* to *H.* 2. has appeard above; and that he acted according to the import of his stile, of *Lord* of *Ireland*, in imposing Laws, and a King upon 'em.

And I would gladly know what *Irish Laws and Customs* he swore to maintain?

Tho, therefore, I am as avers to the common Notions of *Conquest* as this Gentleman, especially to the supposition, that *God*, "in giving one Prince a Conquest over another, THEREBY puts one in possession of the others Dominions, and makes the other's Subjects become his Subjects, or his *Slaves*, as they come in, *upon conditions*, or *at the will of the Conqueror*: Yet I must desire Mr. *M.* to explain those Acts of Parliament made in *Ireland*, which not only seem to import, that the *Crown* and *Kingdom* of *England*, had made an absolute

Vid. *God's ways of disposing of Kingdoms.* P. 20.

The sense of Parliaments in Ireland, *in relation to Conquest.*

solute acquisition of the Land of *Ireland*, but use that scurvy word, *Conquest*.

<small>Stat. Hib. 28 H. 8. c. 3.</small>

An Act, 28 *H.* 8. recites, That the King's Land of *Ireland*, heretofore being inhabited, and *in due obedience unto the King's most noble Progenitors, Kings of* England, *who, in the right of the Crown of* England, *had great Possessions, Rents, and Profits within the same Land;* had grown into great ruin and desolation, for that *great Dominions, Lands, and Possessions, had by the King's Grants,* course of Descents, and otherwise, come to *Noblemen* of *England,* by whose negligence the *wild Irish* got into possession; the *Conquest, and winning whereof,* in the beginning, not only cost the *King's noble Progenitors,* but also those to whom the Lands belong'd, *charges inestimable:* and tho the King's *English Subjects* had valiantly opposed the *Irish,* yet upon their absenting themselves again out of Ireland, *the Natives, from time to time, usurped and encroached upon the King's Dominions;* and particular-ly

<small>F. 64.</small>

ly that the Earl of *Kildare*, with his accomplices, endeavour'd *to take the Land of* Ireland *out of the King's possession, and his Heirs thereof for ever to disherit.*

For these, and divers other hurts and enormities, like to ensue to the Commonweal of the Island; in respect of the *inestimable Charges* which the King had sustained, and apparently had occasion to sustain for, and about *the conquest,* and *recontinuance* of the same, out of his Enemies possession; *tho the King had right to all the Lands and Possessions* there referr'd to, and tho he might justly insist upon the Arrears of two parts of the Land of those who had absented themselves, which might amount to more than the purchase of 'em; it vests in the *King and his Heirs, as in the Right of the Crown of* England, only the Lands of some particular persons.

F. 65.

The Statute of the Queen attainting *Shane Oneile,* speaks of *populous, rich, and well-govern'd Regions, wealthy Subjects, beautiful Cities, and Towns,* of which the *Imperial*

Stat. 11. Eliz. Sef. 3. c. 1.

perial *Crown of* England had, before that time, been *conveniently furnished,* within the *Realm of* Ireland; which after being loft, had been *recontinued* to the Queen's *quiet poſſeſſion.*

But the Rebel, *Shane Oneile,* refuſing the name of *a Subject, and taking upon him,* as it were, the Office of a Prince, had enterprized great *Stirs, Inſurrections,* and horrible *Treaſons,* againſt her *Majeſty,* her *Crown,* and *Dignity;* imagining to deprive her Highneſs, her *Heirs* and *Succeſſors,* from the real and actual poſſeſſion of her *Kingdom* of *Ireland,* her *true, juſt, and ancient Inheritance to her, by ſundry Deſcents, and authentick ſtrong Titles, rightfully and lawfully devolved.*

And having mention'd a Title from *Gurmond* the Son of *Belin,* King of *Great Britain,* ſays,

F. 37.

"Another Title is, as the Clerk
" *Giraldus Cambrenſis* writeth at
" large, of *the Hiſtory of the Conqueſt of* Ireland, by King *H.* 2.
" *your famous Progenitor.*

The Title to the *Land* then recognized,

ependency of Ireland. 51

abundantly strengthned
ed by *Irish* Parliaments
of *J.* 1. and since. In the
nition to *J.* 1. they tell 11 J. c. 1.
ving quench'd the most
nd *universal Rebellion,*
as rais'd in that King-
e suppressing whereof,
'd *parts of the Land,*
rul'd by *Irish* Lords and
d never before receiv'd
I civil Government of
re so broken and reduc-
ce, that all the Inhabi-
f did gladly submit
his *Highness's ordinary*
giftrates: which gave
esty *a more entire, abso-*
al possession, than ever
ogenitors had.
being thus brought in-
o the Crown and Laws
K. *James* taking notice
h had been made * af- * 12, 13, 14,
est of that Realm by J. 1. c. 5.
s *Kings of* England, to
istinction between the
he Natives of the *Irish*
he had then taken 'em
    D 2   all

The History and Reasons

all into his protection, and that they lived *under one Law, as dutiful Subjects* of their *Sovereign Lord and Monarch*, repeals those dividing Laws.

After this the *Irish* Parliament granted C. 1. four Subsidies, *rightly considering the vast, and almost infinite expence of Men, Mony, Victuals, and Arms, sent out of* England *thither, by the King and his Royal Progenitors, for reducing that Kingdom into the happy condition wherein it then stood.*

And sutably to the import of the word *Conquest*, Acts of Parliament of that Kingdom, in the Reign of that King, shew that the Titles to Lands of the *English Plantation*, or which they from time to time gain'd from the *Irish*, were enjoy'd by Grant from the Crown: and for securing the Estates to *Undertakers, Servitors, Natives*, and *others*, all the Lands in several Counties, commonly call'd *Plantation Lands*, were vested in the King, his *Heirs* and *Successors*, in right of *the Imperial* Crown of *England* and *Ireland*.

* *Act for Subsidies,* 11 C. 1.

10 C. 1. Sef. 1. c. 3. and Sef. 3. c. 3.

Nota, But one *Imperial Crown.*

The Stat. 14 & 15. C. 2. holds the *Irish* Rebels to be subdued and conquer'd Enemies, and therefore vests all their Lands in the *Crown* of *England*, in order to make satisfaction to the *Protestant Adventurers*, for the reducing that Kingdom to its due obedience, and to enable the Crown to extend Grace to such as should be held deserving of it; Reprisals being first made to the Protestant Proprietors.

14 & 15 C. 2.

Tho, therefore, I am far from admiring the Lord *Coke*'s reasoning in *Calvin*'s Case; I may here subjoin part of Mr. *M*'s reflection upon him, and refer him to the *Irish Acts of Parliament* to qualify his Censure of the Ld *Coke*'s restriction of the Opinion in the *Year-book*, 2 R. 2. that the *Irish* are not bound by Statutes made in *England*, because they have no *Knights of Parliament* here; which, says the Lord *Coke*, *is to be understood, unless they be specially named.* To this assertion Mr. *Molineux* admits he gives *colour of reason*, by saying, "That tho *Ireland* be a distinct Dominion from *England*, yet the Ti-

Non hic habent Milites Parliamenti.

P. 117.

"tle

"tle thereof being by *Conquest*, the same by *Judgment of Law*, might by express words be bound by the Parliaments of *England*.

P. 117.

To confound the Lord *Coke*, I "would fain know, says this Gentleman, what the Lord *Coke* means by *Judgment of Law:* Whether he means the Law of Nature and Reason, or of Nations, or the Civil Laws of our Commonwealths? For answer to which I need at present only ask him, what sort of Law he takes the above-cited Statutes of *Ireland* to be? and shall afterwards shew that they have all along submitted to such a Conquest, or Acquisition, as gives a Right to the imposing of Laws.

P. 118.
Of Mr. M's comparison between Scotland and Ireland; and of the Annexation of Ireland to the Crown of England.

3. But since he is pleas'd to say, As *Scotland*, tho the King's Subjects, *claims an exemption from all Laws but what they assent to in Parliament*; so we think this our Right also: and going upon the supposition of *Ireland*, being a Kingdom as distinct from *England* as *Scotland*, he frames an Objection, that however they may be restrain'd by War from doing

ing what may be to the prejudice of *England*, the stronger Nation: If this may be, he asks, why does it not operate in the same manner between *England* and *Scotland*, and consequently in like manner draw after it *England*'s binding *Scotland* by their Laws at *Westminster*?   P. 147.

As to *Scotland*, not here to enter into the Dispute between the Lord *Coke* and the rest of the Judges, who resolv'd *Calvin*'s Case, and the House of Commons of that time; nor yet, into the Question concerning the *Scotch Homage*, whether 'twas for the Kingdom of *Scotland*, or only for some Lands which their Kings held of the Crown of *England*: 'Tis enough to observe, that during the *Heptarchy* here we often had one King, who was *Rex primus*, to whom the others were *Homagers*, and obedient in the Wars for *common Defence* of the Island; yet each King had his distinct Regalities, and the Countrys their several Laws and Customs, and *distinct Legislatures* for Lands, and other Rights and Things within themselves.   Vid. Moor's Rep.

Thus

This 'twas easy to conceive that *Scotland* had; and thus, both there and here, under the *Heptarchy*, the several Kingdoms, notwithstanding Homage to one King who had the *Primacy*, were under separate Allegiances, as the respective Subjects were not bound to the same Laws; tho the States of the Kingdom did Homage as well as the King. When the Right to the Crown of *Scotland* came afterwards in *J.* 1. to be in the same Person who had the Crown of *England*, and that without any new Acquisition by the Crown or Kingdom of *England*, there was (*a*) no *merger* of the less Crown: and 'tis certain that in the Judgment of Law, *Palatinates* fallen to the Crown continue distinct Royalties.

But if, for the keeping a Kingdom distinct, whether in the Person of the same King, or as an Appendant to his Imperial Crown (*b*), a distinct Legislature is necessary as well as a distinct Jurisdiction; then *Wales*, which in many of our Statutes is call'd a Dominion, was no di-

Vid. Ben. Ab. in Bib. Cot. de Homagio Regis Scot. H. 2.

(*a*) Vid. Answ. to C. J. Herbert on the dispensing Power; and particularly the Sherivalty of the County of N. for which some have supposed that the Statute in that case was dispensed with. A Comparison between Ireland and Wales.
(*b*) Mr. M. p. 165.

of the Dependency of Ireland.

distinct Dominion, or Principality; if it at any time continued in the Crown, without having Parliaments of their own, or being represented here, by Members of their own chusing: but thus it was with *Wales* from the 12*th* (*c*) of *E.* 1. to the 34*th* of *H.* 8. in right of *E.* 1*st*'s Conquest, as Sir *John Davis*, or the Judges in his time call the Acquisition of that Dominion; and as 'tis there; " *E.* 1. changed " their Laws and Customs as he " had express'd in his Charter, or " the Statute of *Rutland* which fol- " lows:

(*c*) 34 H. 8. c. 13.

Divinâ providentiâ terram Walliæ cum incolis suis prius nobis jure feodali subjectam, in proprietatis nostræ dominium totaliter & cum integritate convertit, & coronæ regni nostræ annexit.	*By the Divine Providence the Land of Wales, with its Inhabitants, before subject to us by feudal Right, we have turn'd wholly and entirely into the Dominion of our Propriety, and annexed it to the Crown of our Kingdom.*

Davis's Rep. f. 41. b.

Should be in the plural number.

And as to their Laws and Customs;

Quas-

Quasdam de consilio procerum regni nostri delevimus, quasdam permisimus, quasdam correximus, ac etiam quasdam alias adjiciendas & faciendas decrevimus.	*Some, by the Counsel of the Peers of our Kingdom, we have abrogated, some we have permitted, some we have corrected, and besides some others we have added and decreed to be put in execution.*

Here is a Title, understood at that time, of taking a Forfeiture for Rebellion against the Lord of the Fee; and in consequence of this the King and his Peers, in Parliaments, took upon them to exercise a Legislative Power over *Wales*.

But notwithstanding that *Wales* was thus united and annexed to the Imperial Crown of *England*, and absolutely subjected to its Legislature, yet, as is held in *Davis*'s Reports, this Principality of *Wales*, not being govern'd by the common Law, was a Dominion by it self, and had its proper Laws and Customs.

<small>Davis f. 67. le Case del County Palatine.</small>

That Report shews *Wales*, by reason of these different Laws and Customs,

Customs, to be more distinct and separate from the Kingdom of *England*, than *Ireland* is; and that a Tenure of the Prince of *Wales* should not after its reduction under the Subjection of *England*, become a Tenure of the Crown in chief, but that it should be so in relation to Tenures of a County *Palatine* in *Ireland*, as well as *England*, because such a County in either Land was originally a parcel of the Realm, "and derived from the Crown, and "was always govern'd by the Law "of *England*; and the Lands there "were held by Services and Te- "nures, of which the common "Law takes notice, altho the Lords "have a separate Jurisdiction, and "Seigniory separate from the "Crown. But that Tenure in Chief in *Ireland*, as well as *England*, could be no other than of the Crown of *England*, appears not only by the Grants to the *Electors Palatine*, or *Lords Marchers* of *Ireland*, but in that *Ireland* was not raised into a Kingdom till *H.* 8's time.

F. 67.

The mention of *Palatinates* may
well

Comparison between Ireland and the County Palatine of Chester.

well occasion a Comparison between the Land of *Ireland*, and the *County Palatine* of *Chester*, a distinct Royalty in the Principality of *Wales*: that had its Parliaments within it self, as 'tis very probable, from before the time of *W.* 1. it being certain, that *Hugh Lupus* enjoyed that Earldom by Judgment of the Lords, if not the Great Council in the time of *W.* 1. and their Parliaments may be traced from within the time of *H.* 3. downwards to their first having Representatives in Parliaments of the Kingdom, 34 *H.* 8.

Rot. Pat. 9. H. 3. m. 9. d.
Rot. Pat. 44. H. 3. m. 1. d.
Pat. 6. E. 1. m. 6. de 15ma in Com. Cestr.
Pat. 20. E. 1. m. 6. de 15ma Regi, &c.

Their *provincial Parliaments* were chiefly, if not only, for the granting Aids to the Crown: but notwithstanding their being represented in Parliaments at home, yet Laws were made here in the superior Parliament, for the governing the Inhabitants of the County of *Chester*.

P. 148. Some object, that Ireland is to be look'd upon only as a Colony from England.

Now, without considering whether *Cheshire* was a Colony from *England*, or from *Wales*, or mix'd, or else a place exempt without regard to the being any Colony; I may well hold, that tho from before the time

of the Dependency of Ireland.

time of *W.* 1. they had the privilege of being tax'd only by themselves, or with their own Consent: yet their Parliament was subordinate to the Great Council of the Kingdom of *England*; and 'twas no violation of the Right of their Parliament, for the National Council to give them Laws for their better Government, and to restrain 'em from acting to the prejudice of the Crown and Kingdom of *England*: neither was this any diminution to the Prerogative of the Crown. The instance of *Chester* I may well bring to this point, being authorized by the Learned Judg *Shardlow* in the time of *E.* 2.

In an Action of Debt in the King's-Bench here, upon a Bond seal'd at *Chester*, that learned Judg says; "*Chester* is out of our Jurisdiction here, insomuch that there is not any Minister in that County answerable here for what he has done. Of a Deed done out of the Jurisdiction here, or out of the Realm, as at *Paris*, or elsewhere beyond Sea, I ought not to

Year-book of E. 2. f. 613.

" to anfwer. The Counfel urges, that "*the Power here extends through-*
" *out the Realm of* England, *and to*
" *a Deed done within the Realm*
" *of England you ought to anfwer;*
" *and Chefter is within England.*

But *Shardlow* infifts upon his former Judgment, and adds, "IRE-
" LAND IS WITHIN THE REALM;
" and to a Deed committed there,
" *I fhall not anfwer here.* Alfo *Durefm*
" is within *England*, yet I fhall not
" anfwer at all here; *becaufe the*
" *Court cannot try the Fact if de-*
" *nied.*

This fhews plainly, that at that time *Ireland* was as much part of this Realm as *Chefter*; that the diftinction of Jurifdictions was not for want of Superiority. This has been maintain'd over * *Chefter* and *Ireland*, by Writs of Error upon Judgments in Law. The reafon of which is given by Chief † Juftice *Vaughan*, that *otherwife they may infenfibly alter the Law appointed, or permitted, or give judgment to the leffening the Superiority.*

* 19 H. 6.
F. 12. b.
4. Inft. F. 212.

† Vaughan's Rep.

Mr.

endency of Ireland.

eux will have it, that
al of a Judgment from
ench of *Ireland*, by Writ
to the *King's Bench* of
; not infer the ſubordi-
land to the Kingdom

but that this was a
inted by an Act of Par-
eland, which is loſt a-
: number of other Acts
want for the ſpace of
t one time, and 120 at
T'is eaſily ſuppoſed by
ey had Parliaments of
for the moſt of thoſe
others will believe that
nerally governed by the
land, according to the
heir ſubmiſſion to *H*. 2.
rpretation then put up-
niſſion. But methinks
his Argument, in rela-
rdinary *Juriſdictions* the
) of *England* exerciſes o-
reland, is not to be fear'd.
eaſed to ſay, *erroneous*
ight have been removed
id *into the King's Court
for ſo certainly it muſt
be*

* *Of the Juriſ-
diction of the
King's Bench
of England o-
ver that of
Ireland.*
P. 13.
Vib. ib. *the
Lord* Coke,
*ſeems to infer
from the ſubor-
dination,* &c.

P. 13.
*Of the ordinary
Juriſdiction of
the K's Bench
of England o-
ver that of
Ireland.*

be since the Court travelled with the *King*. For which I need only mind him of his own quotation of * Sir *Richard Pembrough*'s Case: according to which, for the King to have required the attendance there of the *Tenants in chief*, who were the Judges in his Court here, would have bin a banishment: But 'tis certain this could be no part of their Duty declared by the constitutions of *Clarendon*, 10 *H*. 2. in affirmance of the antient customs of the *Realm* of *England*, under that clause which requires 'em to be at the *Trials and Judgments of the King's Courts*.

* P. 164, 165.

Interesse judiciis Curiæ Regis.

Besides, I shall shew, that the *King's Court* in *England* (which when not meant of the Parliament, did manifestly in those antient times relate either to a *Counsel chosen in Parliament*, and acting out of it by Authority from thence, or to the Body of the Tenants in chief, the *Great Lords*, for whose easing themselves of such troublesome attendances, the later Jurisdiction of the present *King's Bench* has sprung up) was possess'd of the Superiority of
ordinary

of the Dependency of Ireland.

ordinary Jurisdiction over *Ireland*, before Mr. *M.* can shew that they had any Acts made in *Ireland* of any kind, except that wherein they first gave themselves up to obey and depend on the *English Legislature*; and unless they can produce Acts of their Parliaments for raising Aids to the *Crown* of *England*.

In * the 37*th* of *H.* 3. one *Baret* complain'd to the King of injustice done him by Justices itinerant at *Limbrick*.

* Rot. Clauf. 37 H. 3. m. 4. d. Hibn.

Upon which the Justices of *Ireland* were commanded to send the Record before the King.

Et mandatum est Justiciariis Hiberniæ quod recorda cum omnibus adminiculis coram eo venire faciant.

Where the Record was commanded hither, *per saltum*, without any regard to the *King's Bench* of *Ireland*.

And another Record in the same year before *Shardlow*, and other Justices at *Dublin*, as I take it, of the *Common Pleas* there, was, by Writ of Error from hence, transmitted to the *Justice* of *Ireland*: Without which it seems he was then held to have no Authority to proceed in *Ireland*.

Rot. Clauf. 37 H. 3. m.15.

E   In

Recorda penes Remem. in scaccar. Placita coram Rege 20 E. 1. Vid. inf. of Petitions in Parl. Temp. E. 1.

In the 20*th* of *E.* 1. a Writ of Error had removed out of *Ireland* a Record of a Judgment of Felony: Which, indeed, was remanded; not for want of Jurisdiction to correct the Error of the Judges in *Ireland:* But,

1. Because there was no notice to the King's Attorney General for *Ireland:* or at least, he did not attend.

2. Because 'twas a question of Fact.

Quia nullus venit ex parte Regis ad sequendum pro ipso, qui veritatem sciverit, ideo hæc non potest ad examinationem; set magis expedit domino Regi, quòd in partibus Hiberniæ, ubi feloniæ præd. perpetrari debent, examinentur, & modo debito terminentur.

Because no body who may know the truth, comes of the part of the King to prosecute for him: Therefore this cannot proceed to examination: but 'tis expedient for the King, that the said Felonies should be examined, and duly determined in Ireland, where the said Felonies are suppos'd to have been committed.

of the Dependency of Ireland.

P. 133.

However Mr. *M.* conceives it "*manifest,* that the *Jurisdiction* of "the *King's Bench* in *England* over 'a Judgment in the *King's Bench* 'of *Ireland,* dos not proceed from "any *subordination* of one Kingdom to the other; because the 'Judges in *England* ought, and "always do judg according to the 'Laws and Customs of *Ireland,* 'and not according to the Laws 'and Customs of *England,* any otherwise than as these may be of force in *Ireland.* But,

P. 132.

1. 'Tis evident that the Judges either will, nor can judg according to any Law or Custom [of] *Ireland*, which is contrary to the Rules of our Law, or which has not been allowed there as [a] way prejudicial to the Law here: according to his instance of a *Declaration for an Acre of Bog, a word* not *known in* England; but well enough understood in *Ireland.* Which I may answer with a parallel case lately adjudged in the *Exchequer* of *England.*

P. 133.

E 2 One

One having spoken scandalous *welsh words* in *Wales*, or in a part of *England* where the *Welsh* Tongue is used, was libel'd against in the Ecclesiastical Court there: Upon which the Court of *Exchequer* was moved for a Prohibition, because the Words were *insensible*, and of no signification: But no Prohibition was granted, because they were understood where they were spoken. And thus 'tis in relation to the particular Instances of Mannors, or inferiour Courts. Therefore,

2. By the same reason, that the judging according to the Law used in *Ireland* would imply, that there is no Subordination, 'twill follow that the Inferior Courts in *England* are not *subordinate* to the Courts of *Westminster-Hall*: and I may add, neither is the *King's Bench* of *England subordinate* to the House of Lords.

The ordinary Jurisdiction of the Lords, and the King's Bench, an incident to the Superiority of the Crown of England.
* P. 3.

As to the question of their Jurisdiction, occasioned, as Mr. *M'* * Margin has it, by the Case of the Bishop of *Derry*, I need say little here, referring him to the Judg

of the Dependency of Ireland.

ment of the *Lords*, and to that exercice of the Judicial Power, which I shall have an opportunity of shewing in the Reign of *E.* 1.

But as to his supposed *clear* Argument against the *subordination*, from the Lords doing nothing upon the Petition of the Prior of *Lanthony*, who appeal'd to the Parliament of *England*, from a refusal of the *King's Bench* here to meddle with a Judgment which had pass'd in the Parliament of *Ireland*: P. 125, 126. Rot. Parl. 8 H. 6.

'Twill admit of several Answers;

1. This came not before the Lords by Writ of Error, or by Appeal from the Lords of *Ireland*; but as a complaint of the *King's Bench* here.

2. This was after the Charter which I shall afterwards shew, placing a judicial Power to some purposes in their *Parliaments*: But whether they exceeded that Authority, 'twas not for the *King's Bench* to judg, but for that Power from whence their Charter was derived.

3. This

3. This Petition seems either to have come too late, or to have been waved: for if it had fallen under consideration, 'tis probable that some Answer to it could have been endors'd, as was usual in former times.

But that the *ordinary Jurisdiction* both of the Lords in Parliament, and of the *King's-Bench* here, is but an incident to the Superiority of the Crown of *England*, will be much clearer than any thing Mr. *M.* has urged. And whatever Mr. *M.* conceives, the Annexation of *Ireland* to the Crown of *England*, will sufficiently manifest the *Subordination*; tho he, supposing that this was done by the Irish Statute, which annexes it as a Kingdom, with others which declare it annex'd as a *Land* or *Dominion* of a lower Character, conceives " little more is effected by " these Statutes, than that *Ireland* " shall not be aliened or separated " from the King of *England*, who " cannot hereby dispose of it, otherwise " than in legal Succession along " with *England*; and that " who-

Of the Annexation of Ireland *to the Crown of* England.
P. 41, 42.

P. 44.

of the Dependency of Ireland.

"whoever is King of *England,* is
"*ipso facto* King of *Ireland.*

But if these Statutes, bating the name of Kingdom (which the Parliament of *England* afterwards gave them) are only declaratory of the antient Right of the Crown of *England;* then I may well hold, that there is not so much effected by these Statutes, as he yields, it being only the operation of Law. And if by operation of Law a King of *England,* tho not succeeding by a strict Right of Descent, but by the Choice or Declaration of the States of this Realm is *ipso facto* King or Lord of *Ireland,* I would gladly know how that Kingdom or Land, which he owns to be thus inseparably annex'd to the Imperial Crown of *England,* can be a compleat Kingdom? And since he is pleas'd to ask, whether *multitudes of Acts of Parliament, both of* England *and* Ireland, *have not declared* Ireland *a compleat Kingdom?* and whether 'tis not stiled in them all, *the Kingdom or Realm of* Ireland? -

P. 127.
P. 149.
Vid. Davis Rep. f. 61. *citing* 28 H. 8. c. 2. La corone d' engleterre en plusors auters Acts de Parl. est appel. Imperial Crown, & la corone de Ireland est appendant, a ceo 28 H. 8. c. 20. & unite & knit al. Imperial corone D' engleterre, 33 H. 1. c. 1.

I would entreat the favour of him, to shew me one Act of Parliament of either Kingdom, which says, or all Circumstances consider'd implies, that *Ireland* is a *compleat Kingdom*: or that ever any Parliament of their own held it to be advanced to the Dignity of a Kingdom, before 33 *H*. 8. tho, as they acknowledg, the Kings of *England* had Kingly Power there long before.

<small>33 H. 8. c. 1.</small>

I must own, that as the name of *King* was in *H*. 8's time thought requisite to charm the *wild Irish* into Obedience; so in Queen (*a*) *Elizabeth*'s time, *Imperial Crown* was thought to make a conquering Sound: but this was never ascribed to it by any Parliament of *England*; nor, that I can find, even of *Ireland*, before her Reign or since.

<small>(*a*) 2 Eliz.c.1, & c. 2.</small>

But the *one Imperial Crown*, upon which *Ireland* has been, and still is, dependent, is the Crown of *England*: for this the Statute of *Ireland*, before that was made a Kingdom, is express, having these words;

" Call-

of the Dependency of Ireland.

" Calling to our remembrance the 28 H. 8. c. 2.
" great Divisions which in time
" past have been, by reason of seve-
" ral Titles pretended to the Impe-
" rial Crown of the Realm of *Eng-*
" *land*, whereunto this your Land
" of *Ireland* is appending, and be-
" longing.

So another in the same Year.
" Forasmuch as this Land of *Ire-* 28 H. 8. c. 5.
" *land* is depending, and belonging,
" justly and rightfully to the Impe-
" rial Crown of *England*; it enacts, that the King, his Heirs and
Successors, Kings of the Realm of
England, and Lords of this said
Land of *Ireland*, shall have and enjoy, *annexed and united to the Impe-*
rial Crown of England, all Honours,
Dignities, Pre-eminencies and Authorities, *&c.* belonging to the
Church of *Ireland*.

If Mr. *Molineux* observes duly, P. 166.
Ireland has all these Imperial Rights
declared in the Irish Statute, 33
H. 8. *c.* 1. but I cannot find by what
Rule he infers this from an Act of
Parliament, which is express, that
the King of *England* shall have the
Name,

Name, Stile, Title and Honour of King of *Ireland*, with all manner of Preheminencies, *&c.* as united and knit to the Imperial Crown of the Realm of *England*.

Indeed it shews, that under the name of *Lord*, the King had the same Authority; but the name of *King* was thought likely to be more prevalent with the Irish Men, and Inhabitants within that Realm.

11 Jac. 1. c. 1. The Statute, 11 *Jac.* 1. declares him King of *England, Scotland, France,* and *Ireland*, by God's Goodness, and Right of Descent under one Imperial Crown.

10 C. 1. Seff. 3. c. 3. And the Statute, 10 *C.* 1. calls this the Imperial Crown of *England* and *Ireland:* And indeed Mr. *Molineux* would do well to shew that ever any of our Kings took any Coronation Oath for *Ireland*, otherwise than as Kings of *England*.

And yet I know not what he may do when his hand's in; since he has the Art to transubstantiate their Recital of an Act of Parliament in *England*, which declares that
Popes

of the Dependency of Ireland.   75

Popes had usurped an Authority in derogation of the Right of the Imperial Crown of the Realm of *England*; recognizing no Superiour under God but only the King, and being free from Subjection to any Man's Laws, but only such as have been devised, made and ordain'd within the Realm of *England*; or to such other as, by sufferance of the King and his Progenitors, the People of the Realm of *England* had taken at their free Liberty, *by their own Consent, to be used among them, and have bound themselves by long Custom to the observance of the same*; To infer that 'tis thus with *Ireland*, because the enacting part of that Statute which has this Recital is promulged for a Law in *Ireland*, is to suppose *Ireland* to be turned into *England*; and that the Commissioners, who are by virtue of that Act and the Great Seal, to exercise that Ecclesiastical Jurisdiction which the Statute in *England* placed in the See of *Canterbury*, are become English Archbishops.

Q. *Whether of* England *or* Ireland, *neither being named.*

And

And with the like way of reasoning he would infer, that Acts of *Recognition* in *England* are of no Force in *Ireland*, till the Irish have recognized the same King; and yet

P. 55.

confesses, " That whoever is King
" of *England* is *ipso facto* King of
" *Ireland*, and the Subjects are ob-
" liged to obey him as their Leige

P. 127.

" Lord: That they in *Ireland* are
" so annexed to *England*, that the
" Kings and Queens of *England* are
" by undoubted Right *ipso facto*
" Kings and Queens of *Ireland*. To

P. 157.

use Mr. *M*'s own Expression, *I am sure there's an end of all Speech*, if he does not confess, that a Prince rightfully possest of the English Throne, is thereby King of *Ireland*, before any Recognition made by a Parlia-

P. 127.

ment there: and yet notwithstanding this generous Concession, he immediately subjoins;

" And from hence we may rea-
" sonably conclude, that if any
" Acts of Parliament made in *Eng-*
" *land* should be of force in *Ireland*,
" before they are receiv'd there in
" Parliament, they should be more
" espe-

" especially such Acts as relate to
" the Succession and Settlement of
" the Crown, and Recognition of
" the King's Title thereto, and the
" Power and Jurisdiction of the
" King. And yet we find in the
" Irish Statutes, 28 *H.* 8. *c.* 2. *An*
" *Act for the Succession of the King,*
" *and Queen* Ann. And another,
" *c.* 5. declaring the *King to be su-*
" *preme Head of the Church of* Ire-
" land. Both which Acts had for-
" merly pass'd in the Parliament of
" *England.* So likewise we find
" amongst the Irish Statutes, Acts
" of Recognition of the King's Ti-
" tle to *Ireland* in the Reigns of
" *H.* 8. Queen *Elizabeth,* King
" *Charles* 2. K. *William* and Q. *Ma-*
" *ry*: by which it appears, *that* Ire-
" land, *tho annexed to the Crown of*
" *England, has always been look'd*
" *upon to be a Kingdom compleat*
" *within it self, and to have all Ju-*
" *risdiction to an absolute Kingdom,*
" *belonging, and subordinate to no*
" *Legislative Authority on Earth.*
" Tho 'tis to be noted, those Eng-
" lish Acts relating to the Suc-
" cession

P. 128.

"cession and Recognition of the
" King's Title, do particularly
" name *Ireland.*

Before I enter into the enquiry how this can be made consistent with a Kingship *ipso facto* before the Recognition in *Ireland*; 'twill be requisite to inform him, that we have had Settlements of the Crown by Acts of Parliament here, which never were formally received by any Parliament in *Ireland*; and yet such Act of Parliament here has ever been held to bind *Ireland*, tho 'twas not expresly named; and that tho the Settlement has carried the Crown from the elder Branch of the Royal Family: for instance, 7 *H.* 4. at the request of the Lords and Commons in Parliament, 'twas enacted, " That the Inheritance
" of the Crown and of the Realms
" of *England* and *France*, and of
" all other the King's *Seigniories*
" or Lordships beyond Sea, with
" the appurtenances, be put and
" remain in the Person of the said
" King, and the Heirs of his Body
" issuing; and 'twas ordain'd, esta-
" blished,

Vid. the printed Statute-Book ending with R. 3. *and Reflections upon a treasonable Opinion against signing the Association.*

of the Dependency of Ireland.   79

'blished, pronounced, expressed,
'and declared, that Prince *Henry*,
'the King's eldest Son, *be Heir ap-*
'*parent*, to succeed him in the
'said *Crown*, Realms, and Seignio-
'ries; to have them with all their
'Appurtenances, after the King's
'decease to the Prince and the
'Heirs of his Body; with Re-
'mainders over, to the King's 2*d*
'and 3*d* Sons, and the Heirs of
'their respective Bodies succes-
'sively.

And according to this Form 1 *H.* *In the beginning*
'"'twas ordain'd, established, and *of the Statutes*
'enacted, by Authority of Parlia- *of H. 7. in*
'ment, that the Inheritances of *French.*
'the Crowns of the Realms of
'*England* and *France*, with all the
'preheminence and dignity Royal
'to the same appertaining, and
'all other *Seigniories* belonging to
'the King beyond Sea, with the
'Appurtenances in any manner
'due to them, or appertaining, do
'stand and remain in the most no-
'ble Person of their said Sovereign
'Lord *H.* 7. and the Heirs of his
'Body lawfully issuing for ever,
"with

" with the Grace of God to endure,
" and in no other Persons.

Not to trouble Mr. *M.* with an enquiry, whether these, or any other Acts of Parliament in *England* of former Reigns, united *Ireland* to *England*, otherwise than as they declared their intention for that Seigniory, or Dominion, to go along with the Government of *England*; or what Act of Parliament in *Ireland*, since the first submission to *H.* 2. created an Annexation of the Land of *Ireland* to the Crown of *England*; I must entreat him to explain,

How it should come to pass, that the King of *England, ipso facto,* by his being made King here, is King of *Ireland*; and yet that those Acts of Parliament here, by which the King is declared King, without and against a strict course of descent, are of no *force* till the King is recognized by Act of Parliament in *Ireland*?

If a *King* of *England, as such,* is *ipso facto* King of *Ireland*, is he not so before any Act of Recognition there? And if so, what can that,

of the Dependency of Ireland.

that, or other Acts repeating the Laws made in *England*, signify more, than a full publication of what was the Law before?

If the *Election*, or Declaration of a King, by a Parliament in *England*, gives a Law in this matter to *Ireland*; and such a King is to be obey'd by virtue of that Law, *ipso facto*, before he is received and acknowledged by a Parliament in *Ireland*; do their subsequent Recognitions in the least infer that *Ireland* is a *compleat Kingdom*?

Is it any better than a Contradiction to hold, that a King of *England*, as created or declared in a Parliament of *England*, is thereby, or at the same instant, King of *Ireland*; and yet that *Ireland* is a Kingdom so compleat in it self, that he is no King till the Act of Parliament creating or declaring him King, is confirm'd by a Parliament in *Ireland*? Or take it the other way;

No Act of Parliament in *England* is of any force till confirmed in *Ireland*; and yet a King declared by a Parliament of *England*, tho he was not

P. 128.

King before such declaration, is thereby, or *ipso facto*, King of *Ireland*: that is, an Act of Parliament of *England* is not of force in *Ireland* till confirm'd there; and yet 'tis of force *ipso facto* by the being enacted here.

Does it not therefore follow, that such an annexation of *Ireland* to the Crown of *England*, as makes the King of *England, ipso facto* King of *Ireland*, destroys the supposition that their Parliaments have Authority to confirm or reject Laws made by the *Legislature* in *England*? Or otherwise, that the supposition of such an Authority in the Parliament of *Ireland*, destroys that annexation which Mr. *M.* himself yields?

Further yet 'twill appear, that, even after a Parliament of *Ireland* had, as far as it could, annex'd that *Land*, as a *Kingdom*, to the *Imperial Crown* of *England*; an Annexation here was requisite, for the ratifying what had been done in *Ireland*.

Stat. 34 & 35 H. 8. c. 3.

Therefore, 34 and 35 *H.* 8. an Act was made by the Parliament of *England*, for *ratification of the King's Majesty's Stile*; by the King, with

of the Dependency of Ireland.

with the *aſſent of the Lords Spiritual, and Temporal, and the Commons in that Parliament aſſembled,* and by the Authority of the ſame, enacting that *all and ſingular his Grace's Subjects,* and *Reſiants,* of or within *this his Realm* of *England, Ireland,* and *elſewhere,* with other his *Majeſty's Dominions,* from *thenceforth* accept and take the King's Stile, in manner and form following.

"*H.* 8. by the Grace of God, King
" of *England, France,* and *Ireland,*
" Defender of the Faith, and of the
" *Church* of *England,* and alſo of *Ireland,* in Earth the *ſupream Head.*

And 'tis enacted, that the ſaid ſtile *ſhall be* from thenceforth, by *the Authority aforeſaid, united, and annexed, to the Imperial Crown of his Highneſs's Realm of* England.

This related to all Eccleſiaſtical Power, as well as Civil, in *Ireland,* as well as *England :* In purſuance of this the Statute 1 *Eliz.* for the extinguiſhing all *uſurped,* and *Foreign Power,* and *Authority, Spiritual* and *Temporal,* which had been uſed *within this Realm,* or *any other her Majeſty's*

1 Eliz. c. 1.

...sty's Dominions, or *Countries*, enacts, That no Foreign *Prince*, or *Prelat*, shall enjoy any *Power, Jurisdiction, Superiority, Authority*, or Privilege, *Spiritual*, or *Ecclesiastical*, within *this Realm*, or within *any other her Majesty's Dominions*, or *Countries*; but that such Power, &c. shall be abolished out of *this Realm, and all other her Highness's Dominions*: And that all Power of visiting and correcting for *Heresies & Schism, &c.* shall *for ever, by Authority of that Parliament, be united and annexed to the Imperial Crown of this Realm*: Ecclesiastics were to swear that they would maintain all such *Jurisdiction, Privileges, Preeminence* and *Authority*, as *granted* or *belonging* to the *Queen's Highness, her Heirs and Successors*, or *united to the Imperial Crown of the Realm*. And the Queen is impowred to issue out *Commissions* for *the executing that Act*.

This Statute bound *Ireland*, by plain intention, as that 34 and 35 *H*. 8. did in express words. But Mr. *M.* will have it a mighty Argument, that this was of no force in in *Ireland*, till received by a Parliament there: becaufe after it had bin repealed in *England* by one Act, and another fince the *Revolution* has declared fuch Commiffions to be illegal; yet the *Chancellor*, and others in *Ireland*, have held it to be ftill in force there. But,

1. He ought to have fhewn that the Statute here, repealing fo much of the Statute of the *Queen*; as plainly expreft an intention, that no fuch Commiffion fhould be granted in *Ireland*, as the Statute of the Queen did, that *Ireland* fhould be fubject to *the fame Ecclefiaftical Authority*, and *in the fame manner* that *England* was: nor is it to any purpofe for him to cite the Declarations in the late Statute of the illegality of fuch Commiffions; unlefs that Act had damn'd fuch Commiffions, not only as being contrary to the Act of Repeal, but not to be warranted by the *Statute* of the Queen: but then this would have condemned the Refolution which he cites, of the Authority of fuch Commiffions ftill in *Ireland*.

2. Ad-

2. Admit Mr. *M.* should prove, that the Statute made in *England*, taking away the Authority of such *Ecclesiastical Commissions* here, as plainly intended to reach *Ireland*, 'twill afterwards appear, that unless Mr. *M.* shew, that this Act had been *transmitted* to *Ireland*, under the Great Seal of *England*; the supposition that such Commissions may still be legally executed in *Ireland*, will not in the least derogate from the Authority of the Parliament of *England*.

The Power of England not departed from, but duly exercised.

3*dly*, But how contrary his supposal of an independent Authority in the Parliament of *Ireland*, is not only to the Laws of reasoning, but the Authorities of all times, from *H.* 2. downwards, has already appeared in some measure; and may farther by some Authorities out of many, which will manifest, that the Rights of the *Crown* of *England* to impose Laws upon *Ireland*, by virtue of prior *submissions* and *consent*, is so far from being departed from, that 'tis strengthned and confirmed, by long exercice and submission to it.

Mr.

of the Dependency of Ireland.   87

Mr. *M.* considering the State of the Statute-Laws of *England,* under *H.* 2. King *John,* and *H.* 3. agrees, That " *by the Irish voluntary sub-*
" *mission to, and acceptance of the*
" *Laws of* England, *we must repute*
" *them to have submitted themselves*
" *to these likewise, till a regular Le-*
" *gislature was established among them,*
" *in pursuance of that voluntary sub-*
" *mission, and voluntary acceptance.*   P. 57 & 58.

Yet he soon forgets this Concession, and would have it, that the men of *Ireland* were not bound by new Laws, but that the Grants of Liberties from *Edward* the *Confessor*'s time, down to *H.* 3. were only declaratory Laws, *and confirmations one of another;* and *that thus* Ireland *came to be govern'd by one and the same common Law with* England.   P. 62.   P. 63.

I must confess I could not but smile at his Marginal Note upon the proceedings of the Parliament at *Oxford* in the Reign of *H.* 2. *by this* Ireland *made an absolute separate Kingdom:* And in the Body of his Book he says, " *We shall observe that*
" *by this donation of the Kingdom of*   P. 40.

F 4   " Ire-

"Ireland *to King* John, Ireland *was most eminently set apart again as a separate and distinct Kingdom by it self, from the Kingdom of* England; *and did so continue until the Kingdom of* England *descended and came unto King* John.

But to help him to understand this matter, I shall mind him of another passage in *Hen.* II's Reign. As he placed his Son *John* in *Ireland*, he, to secure the Succession of the *Imperial Crown* of *England* to his eldest Son *Henry*, caused him, in a * *Parliament*, to be chosen and made King of *England*, while *Henry* the Father was alive.

* Vid. Bened. Ab. in Bib. Cott. & al. Author.

Now, did the Father by this, separate *England* from his own Jurisdiction? No, certainly; and indeed, in the Oath to the Son, and the homage perform'd, both at the Coronation and afterwards, by the King of *Scots*, there was a particular saving of the *Allegiance* and *Homage* due to the Father.

Thus both *Hoveden* and *Bromton* shew that 'twas, in relation to the constituting *John* King of *Ireland*, as

of the Dependency of Ireland.

as they call him: they are express, that they to whom the Lands of *Ireland* were distributed, in that very *Parliament* which gave *John* his Office and Authority, were sworn to the Father and the Son. And Mr. *M.* might have observ'd, that a Charter pass'd in that Parliament, and cited by Sir *John Davis*, grants to *Hugh de Lacy* large Territories in the County of *Methe*, to hold of *H.* 2. and his Heirs. Whereas if *Ireland* had been given, as Mr. *M.* will have it, to *John, and that thereby 'twas made an absolute Kingdom, separate and wholly independent on* England; The Tenure must have been of *John* and his Heirs. * The Oath of Allegiance, which in those days used to have no mention of Heirs, was to *H.* 2. as King of *England*, and went along with the Crown; but the Tenure reserved, was expresly to the Heirs of *H.* 2. which must relate to the legal Successors to the Crown of *England*; since as King he could have no other Heir.

But as this may manifest, that the Parliament which made *John* King

Davis Rep. F. 64. b.

P. 148.

* Vid. leges W. I. de fide, &c. Regi domino suo.

of

of *Ireland*, design'd him no more than a subordinate and vicarious Authority; 'tis plain he himself did not think he had more: in the Seal which he used, he stiled himself Son * of the King, Lord, or *who is Lord, of* Ireland. Nor is there the least footstep of any Coronation Oath taken by *John* as King of *Ireland*; or that he ever wore an *Irish Crown*.

* Vid. Sandford's *Genealogical Hist.* referring to a Charter in the Cotton Library.
Sigillum Johannis filii Regis, domini Hiberniæ. P. 41.

Notwithstanding that share in the Government of *Ireland* which John had in his Father's life-time; *Ireland* upon the Father's death fell to R. 1. and the Archbishop of *Dublin* was assisting at his first Coronation, before he went to the Holy War: Nor did *John* ever pretend to be King of *Ireland*, while R. 1. lived, more than of *England*; which having attempted, while his Brother was in Foreign parts far remote; upon his Brother's return, he was, by * Parliament, deprived of all his *Honours*, and *Fortune*: And thus, at least, he lost his suppos'd Royalty of *Ireland*, if it did not expire upon the death of *H*. 2. and this

Vid. *Sandford*, sup.
Polidore Virg. f. 255. Habito concilio, &c. de concilii sententia honoribus atq; fortunis privatus. Thorn. int. decem.script. col.1868. Fuit citatus,accusatus, & judicio coram paribus suis per eos legitimè tanquam proditor condemnatus. Mat. Par. Addit. f. 281.

of the Dependency of Ireland.   91

This shews how rightly *Polidore* judged, in calling him (*b*) *Regulus*, or *Viceroy*.

I will therefore admit Mr. *M*'s supposal, that *R*. 1. (*c*) had not died without issue, but *his Progeny had sat on the Throne of* England, *in a continued successim to this day*; but cannot admit the other part of his supposal, that the *same* had been in relation to the *Throne* of *Ireland*; since *John* never had such Throne, either before he was King of *England*, nor after: and therefore I may well conclude, that the *subordination* of *Ireland to the Parliament, or even to the King of* England, need not *arise* from any thing that followed after the *descent of England* to King *John*. Nor indeed was *John* King, either of *England* or *Ireland*, by descent; but that Election of the States of the Kingdom of *England*, which made him their King, preferring him before *Arthur* an elder Brother's Son, drew after it the *Lordship* of *Ireland*, as an Appendant to the Crown of *England*: And however, if *H*. 2. had not sufficiently brought the Irish under the English Laws, *John* did after he came to be King of *England*.

In the 9*th* of his Reign, he (*a*) imposed Laws upon them in a Parliament of *England*; not indeed without the desire and counsel of such English Lords who had Lands in *Ireland*; but then their consent would

(*b*) Ib. F.235. Oxoniam profectus, &c. Johannem fil. totius Hiberniæ regulum facit.

(*c*) P.41,42.

(*a*) Rot. Pat. 9. J. p. 1. m. 2. n. 8. Ad voluntatem & consilium dilector. & fidelium nostror. Com. W. Maresc. & Walt. de Lacey & al. Bar. nostrorum Hiberniæ, qui nobiscum fuerunt in Angl. & per consilium fidelium nostrorum in Angl. Quod latrones Hibern. expellantur de terra nostrâ Hibern. &c.

would have been involved in the consen[t] of the majority here, tho those Lord[s] should have expresly dissented: But th[e] Authority was derived from the consen[t] of the King's *faithful People*, which i[s] mentioned as distinct from the desire o[f] *petition*, which occasioned the Law the[n] made in a Parliament of *England*; for th[e] expelling Thieves and Robbers out o[f] the King's Land of *Ireland*.

For the effectual execution of this A[ct] of Parliament, King *John*'s Expeditio[n] seems to have been undertaken the nex[t] year, when he (b) entirely *subdu'd hi[s] Enemies*; and (c) confiscated the Estate[s] of some of the English great Men in *Ire[-] land*: Which Confiscation seems to hav[e] been after his return to *England*; bu[t] before that, or at some other time i[n] his Reign, he made a Law in *Ireland* which he *commanded to be observed there*. That * *all the Laws and Customs which ar[e] in force in* England, *should be in force i[n]* Ireland; *and that Land be subject to th[e] same Laws, and be govern'd by them*. Thi[s] was before any pretence to their having any Charter for a Parliament, othe[r] than the supposed sending over the *mo[-] dus tenendi Parl.* by *H*. 2. and is befor[e] the time that Mr. *M*. † takes a *regular Le[-] gislature* to have been *established* among them: Therefore according to himself, *we must repute them to have submitted*, not onl[y]

(b) Annales de Margan. Ann. 1210. Jo. 11. f. 14. Hostibus ex voto subactis.
(c) Vid. ib. de Lacy Com. ultorum W. de Breusa Walt. de Lacy, &c. Fecit confiscari omnia bona proscriptorum Principium quæ multa fuerunt in Angl. in Wal. & Hibernia.
* Pat. 30. H. 3. m. 1. Quod omnes leges & consuetudines quæ in Regno Angl. tenentur, in Hibern. teneantur, & eadem ter. eisdem legibus subjaceat, & per easdem regatur, sicut dominus R. J. cum ultimo esset in Hibern. statuit & fieri mandavit.
† P. 58.

of the Dependency of Ireland. 93

only to such Laws as had before that time been made in Parliaments of *England*, but such as should be made, till they of *Ireland* should have the establishment of a *regular Legislature*.

However Mr. *M.* will have it, that *John* gave Laws to *Ireland*, * not as King of England, *but as Lord of* Ireland; and forms a pretty sort of an *Argument* from the stile of *Lord* of *Ireland:* as if this were an *Argument*, that 'tis not dependent upon the Crown of *England*; so excellent a faculty has he of making contraries serve his purpose. But 'tis very unlucky, that *John*'s retaining this stile is not only an Argument that *Ireland* is a Dominion, or *Land*, appendant to the Crown of *England*; but that *John* was ever King † of *Ireland*, which he would certainly have kept up as a distinct Interest, if he ever had such a Title separate from the Crown of *England*.

* P. 54.

†Vid.Rot.Cart. 16. Johannis. Rex Angliæ, Dominus Hibern. Dux Norm. & Aquitaniæ, Comes Audegav.

H. 3. being made K. of *England* by the like choice of the *States*, which preferr'd him before *Arthur*'s Sister, as they did *John* before the Brother; in concurrence with these *States*, truly acted as Lord of *Ireland*, as might be shewn by numerous Instances.

In the 18*th* of his Reign, upon matters signified to him out of *Ireland*, he summoned the *Archbishops, Bishops, Earls, Barons,*

Rot. clauf. 18 H. 3. m.27.

Barons, and all the *great Men,* or *Nobility* of the Kingdom of *England*, to ‖ a Parliament at *London*, to treat about the State of his Kingdom, and of his Land of *Ireland*.

And in the 21 † of his Reign, he sends a Writ to the Archbishops and others * of *Ireland*, acquainting them that by the *common* consent of the *Archbishops*, *Bishops*, *Abbots*, *Earls*, and *Barons* of the Kingdom of *England*, alterations of the Law of *England* were enacted, as to the Limitations of several Writs; which were then required to be observed in *Ireland*, in pursuance of the Statute of *Merton*.

In † the 37*th* of his Reign, an Irish man having pleaded, that he and his Brother, and their Ancestors, had always bin faithful to the Kings of *England*, his Predecessors, and served them in the CONQUEST OF THE IRISH; they are, by peculiar licence under the Great Seal of *England*, admitted to enjoy by descent, as Englishmen. Which was an alteration of the (*a*) Law, and Custom of *Ireland*, as to those particular Persons, without any Act of Parliament there.

Indeed, but four years after 'tis (*b*) recorded, that 'twas (*c*) *long before*, and (*d*) *many Ages past*; which must reach beyond the *Expedition* of *H.*2. provided and

---

‖ Regni nostri Angl.
† Rot. Pat. 21 H. 3. m. 10.
* Ad tractandum nobiscum ibidem super his & aliis statum nostrum, & terræ nostræ Hibern. tangentibus.
† Rot. Clauf. 37 H. 3. m. 15. Firmiter ad fidem & servitium nost. & prædecessor. nostrorum Regum Angl. ad conquestum una cum Anglicis faciend. super Hibernienses.
(*a*) Vid. Sir John Davis de Tanistry.
(*b*) 41 H. 3. m. 11.
(*c*) Dudum.
(*d*) Multis retroactis temporibus, *which Mr. Pryn by mistake has* omnibus.

of the Dependency of Ireland.

[a]nd yielded, by the *assent* and *desire* of the [P]*relats*, and *great Men* of the *Land* of [Ir]*eland*, that they should be bound by [th]e Laws us'd in the Kingdom of *Eng-[la]nd:* Yet the same Record restrains this [to] the *consent* of only the (e) *English* of [th]e *Land* of *Ireland.* However 'tis be-[y]ond dispute that the English Laws, both [m]ade and to be made in *England*, were [th]en held to reach as far as the English [In]terest in the Land of *Ireland:* and this, [ac]cording to the Record 18 *H.* 2. above [re]ferr'd to, was provided *de communi [co]nsilio Regis,* by the *King's Common [Co]uncil:* tho by what Council, it must [ha]ve been *provided*, will more fully ap-[pe]ar afterwards, I may here explain [it] by an Instance in that Reign.

All must agree, that the Provisions of [Ox]*ford*, in the 43*d* of *H.* 3. and referr'd [to] in the Records of the next year, [we]re made in as true a Parliament as a-[ny] in that Reign before the 49*th:* 'tis [ca]ll'd a (g) *Parliament* by good Authors, [an]d the word is used in the Records of [th]e next (a) year, in relation to a meet-[in]g on the Borders of *Wales.* The [(b)] *Ordinances* and *Provisions* made at *Ox*-[for]*d*, were drawn up by 12 chosen by [th]e King, and 12 by the *Commons*; [co]ncerning which the Record has these [wo]rds,

Anno

(e) Omnibus Anglicis terræ Hibern.

* Rot. Pat. 18 H. 3. sup. Rex vult ut de communi consilio Regis provisum est quod omnes leges, &c.

(g) Annales Monast. Burton. f. 411.
(a) Rot. Clauf. 34 H.3. m.7.d.
(b) Annales Burton, sup. In eod. Parl. apud Oxon. xxiv. electi, viz. xii. ex parte domini Regis, & totidem ex parte communitatis.

96   *The History and Reasons*

Rot. Clauf.
44 H. 3. m. 18.
dorso.

Anno ab incarnat. domini 1259. Regni autem H. Regis fil. Regis J. 43. in quindena St. Mic. conven. ipf. domino Rege & magnatibus fuis, de communi confilio & confenfu dictor. Regis & magnatum, factæ funt provifiones per ipfos Regem & Magnates.

In the year from the incarnation of our Lord 1259. but of the Reign of K. Henry, Son of K. John, the 43d, the faid King and his great Men, being affembled in the Quinzifm of St. Michael, Provifions were made by the Common Council, and confent of the faid King, and great men

(c) Rot. Clauf.
44 H. 3. dorf.
m. 18.
(d) Ibid.

And yet fome of the Entries in the fame Roll, mentioning Provifions there made, are, (c) *per magnates nostros qui funt de confilio nostro,* "By our great "Men of our Council. Others, (d) *Per magnates de Confilio meo,* "By the great "Men of our Council. As if 'twas by the fole Authority of the King, and fuch noble Men as were of his Privy or Private Council; when thofe Provifions were certainly made in full Parliament, and this was the Council from whence *Ireland* then receiv'd its Laws.

Object.

P. 45.

However from a Charter in the firft of that King's Reign, Mr. *M.* would infer, that the *English* there had their *independent Parliaments* then eftablifhed, or confirmed, tho he afterwards admits, that during that King's Reign they might

might have been bound by Laws made here for want of a (*a*) regular legiſlature eſtabliſh'd amongſt them.

(*a*) P. 58.

The (*b*) Charter, or rather Writ with which a Charter was ſent, runs thus.

(*b*) P. 47. Pat. 1. H. 3. m. 13. incus.

| Rex Archiepiſc. Epiſc. Abbatibus, Comitibus, Baronibus, Militibus & omnibus fidelibus ſuis per Hiberniam conſtitutis ſalutem. fidelitatem veſtram in Domino commendantes, quam Domino Patri noſtro ſemper exhibuiſtis, & nobis eſtis diebus noſtris exhibituri; volumus quòd in ſignum fidelitatis veſtræ tam præclaræ, tam inſignis, libertatibus Regno noſtro Angliæ à patre noſtro & nobis conceſſis, de gratiâ noſtrâ & dono, in Regno Hiberniæ gaudeatis; quas diſtin- | *The King to the Archbiſhops, Biſhops Earls, Barons, Kts. and all our faithful Subjects conſtituted throughout* Ireland, *Health. Commending your fidelity in the Lord which you always ſhewed to your Lord our Father, and are about to ſhew to us in our days; we will that in ſign of your fidelity ſo remarkable, ſo eminent you enjoy in our Kingdom of* Ireland, *the Liberties granted to our Kingdom of* England, *by our Father & us; which, diſtinctly reduced into Writing, we ſend you, by the* |

G &c

ctè in scriptum reductas, de communi consilio omnium fidel. nostrorum vobis mittimus, signatas Sigillis Domini nostri G. Apostolicæ sedis Legati, & fidelis nostri Comitis Mareschalli, Rectoris nostri & regni nostri; quia sigillum nondum habuimus, easdem processu temporis de Majori consilio proprio Sigillo signatur.

Teste apud Glost. 6. Feb.

Common Counsel of all our faithful People: *Sealed with the Seals of the Lord G. Legate of the Apostolick See, & of our faithful Subject W. Earl Marshal Regent of us and our Kingdom; because we have not yet a Seal, intending in process of time by consent of a greater Counsel to seal them with our own Seal.*

Teste at Gloster, 6. Feb.

Answ. How specious soever this may seem, 'twill neither prove *Ireland* to have been a *Kingdom* so early, nor to have had a grant of the *English Liberties*, in the same manner as the *English* enjoyed them; that is, so as to have no Law imposed upon them without their

their *express and immediate consent*, to that very Law. For,

1. 'Tis not to be suppos'd, but that if *Ireland* had been a *Kingdom* before this Charter, H. 2. and other Kings of *England* would have stiled themselves *Kings of Ireland*, rather than *Lords*, because of the greater Dignity of *Kingship*; unless *Lord* was chosen as implying more absolute Power; which would argue that *Ireland* did not enjoy the *English* Laws with equal Freedom.

2. This Writ mentions no *Liberties* granted to *Ireland*, but what had been (*a*) granted to *England*; which besides the improbability that *Ireland* should 1 H. 3. have a Charter of the (*b*) same form with that which did not pass in *England* till 8 Years after, shews the spuriousness of the suppos'd *Charter* preserved in the (*c*) *red Book* of the *Exchequer* at *Dublin*, as dated the *November* before the Charter sent the 6th. of *February*: and however, the constant (*d*) method of sending Laws from hence to be

(*a*) Regno nostro Angl. concessis.

(*b*) P. 45.

(*c*) P. 46.

(*d*) Vid. Inf. temp. E. 1. & deinceps.

be applyed to the use of the *Irish*, without any alteration; may sufficiently detect that Charter, which has the City of *Dublin* instead of *London*.

P. 45.

3. The method of sending to *Ireland* the Laws made here, besides what appears upon the face of the Record 6. Feb; may satisfie any Body that 'twas only a Writ which went along with a Charter or Charters of Laws, passed in Parliament here.

4. This *Writ* was before any confirmation of the *English Liberties* by *H.* 3. other than general at his Coronation; and therefore bating such Confirmation, the *Charter* of *Liberties* then sent into *Ireland*, must have been *King John*'s which (if it be read according to the due distinction of Periods, and that Translation which the course of Records both before and after enforces, and which the prevalence of Truth has obliged Dr. *Brady* to yeild, to the giving up his whole Controversie with Mr. *Petyt*, and the Author

of the Dependency of Ireland.

thor of *Jani Anglorum Facies Nova*) makes express Provision for the *City of London*, all *Cities*, *Burroughs*, and *Vills* of the Kingdom of *England*, to enjoy all their *Liberties* and *Free-Customs*, and, among the rest, to be of, or to be represented in, the *Common Council* of the Kingdom.

Brady's Append. to his compleat History f. 131. And shall have the Common Advice of the Kingdom concerning the Assessment of their Aids.

But *Ireland* had no *City* of *London* to claim this Privilege; nor could any City of *Ireland* be included, any otherwise than as part of the Kingdom of *England*, and therefore subject to the Laws which should be made here.

2. This could not be as extensive to *Ireland* as 'twas to *England*; since it could not have extended beyond the *English Pale* there, and such particular Districts as enjoy'd the *English Laws*, of *special Favour*.

Therefore the Charter then sent by *H.* 3. could, as to this Matter, be no more than a Memorial of that Supreme Law, according to which, *England*, with all the Dominions belonging to it, was

G 3

The History and Reasons

to be Governed, and an assurance that they should have no Laws imposed upon them, in any other manner, than upon such of the *English* here, as had no Votes in the making Laws. But one end at least of the sending over that Charter must needs have been, suitable to the declared end of a Subsequent sending King *John*'s Charter, when the *Justice of* Ireland was required to Summon, not only the *Great Men*, but the *Free-holders* of every *County*, who after the Laws had been read to them, were to swear to the observance of them; beside which they were to be Proclaim'd in the several *Counties*.

F. 52, 53. *Clauf.*
H. 3. m. 8.

5. Admit the *Charter* sent to *Ireland* 1. *H.* 3. had given the *Irish* Liberty to hold *Parliaments*, with *Representatives* from all parts of that Land, according to the *English* Form; This Liberty was derived from a *Convention* of the *States* of the *Kingdom* of *England*, or *Parliament*, in the Minority of a *King*, who had no Judgment

O

of his own; was under the Government of a Subject whom the *States* had set *over him* and the *Kingdom*; and that *King* was manifestly Chosen by them, to the setting aside *Eleanor*, who had the Right of Descent as far as that could avail: So that, the King could have no pretence to the imaginary divine Right of Succession; and therefore that Charter must have been derived from the Grant of the People of *England*. And besides, the Record shews that this, tho' sent by the advice of all the *King's faithful People*, was thought to want some Formality to make it a *Parliament*: the Assembly in which it was advised, being held by a *Regent*, may be thought to have occasioned the reference to a *greater* (a) or more solemn *Council*: However, such reference shews, that 'twas not their Intention to be concluded by what was then done; and when a Charter is (b) afterwards sent over in full Form, then there's not a word of *Concession*, but an ab-

(a) De Majori consilio.

(b) Vid. Rot. Claus. 12. H. 3. 8. De legibus & consuetud. observandis in Hib. Cited p. 52, 53.

absolute *Command*, that the Laws be *publish'd* and *obey'd*.

However, take the *Charter* sent them 1. *H. 3.* in the utmost extent imaginable, 'tis not to be thought, that while the *English Parliament* gave those of the *English Pale*, or others in *Ireland*, Liberty to hold *Parliaments*, they divested themselves of that Authority by which they gave *such Liberty*.

To use the Words of the great Man *Grotius*,

Grot. de Jure belli & pacis.

Se, per modum legis, id est, per modum superioris, obgare nemo potest. Et hinc est, quod legum Auctores habent jus leges suas mutandi. Potest tamen quis obligari sua lege, non directè sed per reflectionem ex æquitate naturali, quæ partes vult componi ad rationem integri.

No Man can bind himself by way of Law, that is as a Superior. And hence 'tis, that Law-makers have Right to change their Laws. Yet one may be bound by his own Law, not directly, but by reflexion from natural Equity, which requires the parts to be compos'd with respect to the whole.

6. Ad-

of the Dependency of Ireland.

6. Admit the Charter sent 1. *H*. 3. being by consent of the States of the Kingdom of *England*, should be taken for an absolute departure from Power before vested in them; then t ought to be taken *Stricti juris*, and to confer no Right beyond what is express'd: And therefore,

1. The Men of *Ireland* had a Grant only of *such Liberties* as were sent them (a) *distinctly reduced into writing*: And unless the usual Practice of sending over the Laws made here be taken to explain this, or they shew the very Charter then sent; 'tis to be supposed, that *only such Liberties were Expressed* and Granted them, as were proper for an *Appendage to the Crown of* England.

2. If all King *John*'s *Charter* were sent them, (which I may well admit, according to the explanation of the following usage;) unless they can prove, as we can here, that before that time they had *Common Councils of all the Land of* Ireland, for all Matters of

(a) Quas distincte in Scriptum reductas.

of Publick concern, and that the Maxim here had obtain'd there; *Those things which concern all, ought to be treated of by all;* the only end of *Common Councils* of the *Kingdom* of *England*, expressed in *King John's Charter*, being in relation to the principal Grievance about the raising of *Aids* to the Crown; the Grants to *Ireland* could extend no further, than a Liberty to have such a *Council* for the raising Aids.

And there's no doubt, but more Money may be rais'd by such *National Consent*, than can be in the most Arbitrary way: which abates the force of the Argument, from *H.* 3. his desiring the *Archbishops, Bishops, Abbots, Priors, Earls, Barons, Knights, Freemen, Cities,* and *Burroughs of the Land of* Ireland, to Aid him as much as they could, with Men and Money.

And hence, tho' 'twould have been no breach of *King John's* Charter, for the *King* to raise Aids of his *Tenents in Chief*, for making

(b) Quæ omnes tangunt ab omnibus tractari debent.

(c) P. 50, 51. 3. H. 3.

of the Dependency of Ireland.   107

ing *his Eldest Son a Knight,* without calling for them to any *Council*; that being one of the exceptions out of the Liberties expressed in that Charter ; yet *H.* 3. writ to the *Archbishops, Bishops, Abbots, Priors, Earls, Barons, Knights, and all his Freemen of the Land of* Ireland, intreating them to give him *such an Aid.*

Rot. Pat. 37. *H.* 3. pars 2. m. 10.

6. After all, to shew how little there is in his mighty Argument from the Writ 1. *H.* 3. Let him take his choice, either that the *English* in *Ireland* had a *Parliament,* granted, or confirmed to them by the *Charter* sent along with the Writ 1. *H.* 3. or they had not.

If they had, then those Laws which were made here after such Establishment, in pursuance of the desire of them from *Ireland,* shew that neither the *Parliaments* of *England*, nor they of *Ireland* thought they had any Power to make Laws there. If there was no Grant or Confirmation of any *Parliament* there, then the Concession

cession of *English Laws and Liberties*, was no more than a Declaration, that they should be governed by the Laws made, and to be made by *Parliament* in *England*, or receiv'd there by the consent of the People, giving Force and Authority to their own approved Customs.

But since after all Mr. *M.*'s learned Flourishes about the Setling of *Parliaments* in *Ireland*, by the Modus sent over in the time of *H.* 2. and subsequent Grants; he admits that under the 3 Kings, *H.* 2. *King John*, and *H.* 3. *and their Predecessors, we must repute them to have submitted to the Laws made here in those Reigns*, for want of *a regular Legislature establish'd among them*; And since, whatever he admits, there's no Colour of such an Establishment by the end of *H.* 3. Let's see what can be found in the next Reign.

E. 1. having in his absence from *England* upon the Death of *H.* 3. his Father, been *Elected and Declared King of* England, *in a full Con-*

P. 58.

pendency of Ireland.

Of the Authority of the Parliaments of England, exercised over Ireland in the time of E. 1.

...*the States of this King-*
a) Writ sent by those
...*land,* 'tis affirm'd, that
...*ent* of *England,* and
...n or *Lordship* of the
...*nd,* belonged to him by
uccession; not that he
... be King by a meer
...scent, but as the (b) *Ri-*
Coronation of H. 1.
it for Proclaiming the
... in *England,* and Au-
: time shew, the *Ele-*
States of *England* pla-
...e (c) *Inheritance* of the
...efore the *States* of *Eng-*
...to the Subjects of *Ire-*
...ey were bound to take
...1 of *Allegiance* as the
...done; and this is *re-*
...m by the *States* here,
...*reat Seal of England:*
...colour to believe, that
...y Summons to *Ireland*
...1 thence to come to
...*ion;* nor, indeed, was
...or such Summons and
...re that meeting; not-
...; Mr. *M*'s assertion of
this

(a) Rot. Clauf. 1. E. 1. m. 20. De conservatione pacis in Hibern.
(b) Hæreditario judicio.

(c) Clauf. 1. E. 1. m. 11. Quia defuncto jam celebris memoriæ Dom. H. Patre nostro ad nos regni gubernaculum successione hæreditariâ ac Procerum regni voluntate & fidelitate nobis præstita sit de volutum.

this Reign in particular, (a) that the Laws made in *England* and binding them, were *always* enacted *by their proper Representatives*; meaning, *Representatives chosen in Ireland*: the reason for which he there brings from supposed instances in the Reign of *E. 3.* seeming not to rely upon his Quotation from the *white Book* of the *Exchequer* in *Dublin* but the Page before, which 9 *E.*1. mentions (b) Statutes made by the King at *Lincoln*, and others at *York*, with the assent of the *Prelates, Earls, Barons,* and *Commonalty* of his *Kingdom* of *Ireland*. Which, if it implyed the presence of the *Commonalty* of *Ireland*, would be an Argument, that all their Rights were concluded by the *Tenants in chief*, who had Lands in *Ireland*, but were Members of the *English Parliament* by reason of their Interest here: but in truth, this shews no more than that, at the request of those of *Ireland*, the *Parliament* of *England* had enacted those Laws; and the Record in their *white Book* is only a Record of the

trans-

(a) P. 96.

(b) P. 95.

ransmission from hence; and proves that, suitably to the practice both before and after that time, they in *Ireland* had no Parliaments for enacting Laws, but were forc'd to Petition to have them enacted here; and what was enacted upon their *Petition* was truly with their *Assent*. But then the Question will be, whether in the Laws made in that *King*'s Reign with intention to *bind Ireland*, their Consent is generally expressed, or implyed, any otherwise than from the nature of their former *submission* to be govern'd by the *English Laws*. But if our *Acts* of *Parliament*, and *Records* concerning them, are clear in any thing, they certainly are in this, that the Parliament of England then had, and exercis'd, an undoubted Right of binding Ireland, *without their immediate consent by any Representatives chosen there*: Mr. *M.* indeed, tho' as I have before observ'd, he admits that *Ireland* was bound by Acts of Parliament here, till the end of the Reign of *H.* 3. for (4) P. 58.
want

The History and Reasons

want of a *regular legislature among themselves*; yet, suitably to his usual inconsistencies, upon the enquiry, where, (a) and how, the *Statute Laws and Acts of Parliament* made in *England* since the 9th of *H. 3. came to be of force in* Ireland) will have it, that none of them made here, without Representatives chosen in *Ireland*, were binding there, (b) till receiv'd by a suppos'd Parliament 13 E. 2. yet it falls out unluckily, that they have *Statutes* in Print 3 E. 2. which speak not a word of Confirming the Laws before that time made in *England*; and yet no Man will question, but Statute Laws of *England* made in the Reign of E. 1. were a Rule which the Judges in *Ireland* went by, before the time of E. 2. And that all Judgments given in *Ireland* contrary to any Law transmitted thither, under the Great Seal of *England*, must, upon Writs of Error, have been set aside here as Erroneous.

But let's see whether our *Parliaments* in the time of E. 1. had such

(a) P. 63.

(b) P. 64.

of the dependency of Ireland.

h a defference to the *Irish Le-*
ture, or that the *English* in *I-*
nd then made any such pre-
sions as Mr. *M.* advances.

f we Credit *Judge Bolton,* our
tute Westm. 1st. which was 3
1. was first confirm'd in *Ire-*
l 13 *E.* 2. and till then, accord-
to Mr. *M.*'s Inferences from
ir receiving or publishing Laws
de here, that Statute was of
force in *Ireland,* being (d) *In-*
luctory of a new Law in several
ticulars; as among other things,
Subjecting *Franchises* to be seiz-
into the *King's Hands* for de-
lt of pursuing *Felons,* and in
acting, not only the Imprison-
; and Fining Malefactors in *Parks,*
l *Vivaries*, but forcing them
Abjure the Realm, if they could
: find Sureties for their good
haviour.

This Act does not Name *Ire-*
d, but the King *Ordain'd* and
ablish'd it by *His Council,* and
the assent of the *Archbishops,*
bops, Abbots, Priors, Earls, Ba-
is, and all the *Commonalty of*

(d) P: 99 Be-
fore the Year
641. *there was*
no statute made
in England In-
troductory of a
New Law, &c.

H *the*

the *Realm thither Summoned*; fo[r] the mending the Eftate of th[e] *Realm*, for the *Common profit [of] the holy Church of the Realm*; an[d] as *Profitable and Convenient for th[e] whole Realm.*

However that *Ireland*, as pa[rt] of the *Realm*, **was bound by th**[is] Law, and by other Laws mac[e] 11, 12, and 13 *E.* 1. without an[y] regard to *Parliamentary* Confi[r]mations in *Ireland*; and that fo[r] enforcing Obedience to thofe Law[s] 'twas enough to fend them th[i]ther by fome proper *Meſſenge*[r] under the *Great Seal of* Englan[d,] if not without, appears by t[he] Proceedings of the Parliament [at] *Winchester*, holden the *Oct.* after t[he] Parliament of *Weſtm.* 2. (*a*) Me[m.]

(*a*) Pryns Animad. f. 256. 13. *E.* 1. m. 5. de Statutis liberatis. Et Rot. Stat.

quod, *&c.* "Mem. that on *Fri*d[ay] " in the Feaſt of the Exaltati[on] " of the Holy Cross, in the 13t[h] " Year of the King, at *Wincheſt*[er] " there were deliver'd to *Rog*[er] " *Br*e*ton*, Clerk to the Venerab[le] " Father *William*, Biſhop of *Wate*[r] " *ford*, then *Juſtice of Ireland*, ce[r] " tain Statutes, made and prov[ided] " d[e]

of the Dependency of Ireland.

ded by the *King, and His Council*, viz. The Statutes of *Westminster*, made soon after the King's Coronation, and the Statutes of *Gloster*, and *those made for Merchants*, and the Statute of *westm.* provided and made in the *King's Parliament at Easter*; *to be carried to* Ireland, *and there to be Proclaimed and Observed.*

Prynn *omits* Regis *which is in the Record.*

(*b*) In Hiberniam deferenda & ibidem proclamanda & observanda.

It appears that among the Statutes delivered to the *Chief Justices* [c]lerk, in order to their being *published and observed in* Ireland, one [w]as the *Statute concerning Merchants* 12. *E.* 1. for the enforcing [an]d improving a Statute made at [Ac]ton Burnel 11. of that King; [th]at of *Acton Burnel* provides a re[m]edy for Debts to Merchants, to be [pai]d by calling the Debtor before [th]e *Mayor* of *London, York,* or *Bri[sto]l,* or before the *Mayor, and a* [C]lerk to be appointed by the *King*: [w]hich, as it seems, 'twas intended [th]at the King should have Power [to] appoint, in other *Cities* or *Towns* [w]ithin his Kingdom: Accordingly, [th]e Statute 12. *E.* 1. says, the King had

The History and Reasons

had commanded it to be firml[y]
kept (*a*) *throughout his Realm*: an[d]
that Parliament 12. for declarin[g]
or explaining some of the A[r]-
ticles of the former Statute, name[ly]
the *Mayor* of *London*, or the *Chie*[f]
Governour of *that City*, or (*b*) [of]
other good Town: This Statute expresly *Ordains and Establishes*, tha[t]
it be thenceforth held throughou[t]
the *King's* (*c*) *Realm of England, an*[d]
of Ireland: And it enacts the form o[f]
a Writ upon that Statute; which
was to be current in *Ireland* upo[n]
several accounts. 1. By the Letter of that Law, which was ordain'd for the Benefit of Merchant[s]
in *Ireland*, as well as in *Englan*[d].
2. If it had not been named, th[e]
being transmitted to *Ireland* fro[m]
a *Parliament* here, was a sufficien[t]
ground for their observing it.
Such observance was included i[n]
the terms of their Submission, a-
bove one Hundred Years before.
The Writ, without any particular Provision, became a legal an[d]
current Writ in *Ireland*, by virtu[e]

(*a*) En tout son Royaume.

(*b*) Ou de auter bon ville.

(*c*) Per tout son Royaume D'Engleterre & D'Irland.

of the Dependency of Ireland.

[...]f an Act of Parliament here, 30 [H.]3. which, (a) *for the common [p]rofit of the Land of* Ireland, *and u[n]ity of the King's Lands,* provided, [th]at the Common Law Writs [sh]ould have the same currency in [Ir]*eland,* that they have here.

Without enquiring what Re[co]rds they have in *Ireland,* of *Sta[tu]tes Staple* from the 13*th* of *E.* 1. [w]hen this Statute which settled [th]em was sent thither; 'tis certain, [th]at from that time the *English* in [Ir]*eland* were bound by it, and so [he]ld to be in (b) subsequent Sta[tu]tes of this *Realm,* confirming this [St]atute, or supplying its defects.

But what pity 'tis, that neither [Ju]*dge Bolton,* nor Mr. *M.* thought [of] an Act of Parliament in *Ireland* [to] confirm that Statute 12 *E.* 1. [T]his was enacted in the Year 1284. [W]hich was above 350 Years before [th]at fatal *Æra* of Innovations [1]541; from whence it seems Cala[m]ities of all kinds are to be dated. [B]ut, I should think, here is at least [o]ne *positive Precedent* before that [ti]me, *of an English Act of Parliament*

(a) Prynn's Animad. f. 254. 30 H 3. m. 1. Quia pro communi utilitate terræ Hiberniæ & unitate terrarum Regis Rex vult ut de communi consilio Regis provisum est.

(b) Vid. 28 E. 3. & 43 E. 3. c. 1.

P. 99, 103, 105

ment's binding the Kingdom of Ireland.

And to me it seems as plain that in the Judgment of the Parliament 13 *E*. 1. *Ireland*, tho not named, was bound by a Statute made here; for which I shall refer him to the Interpretation there made of the extent of the Statute of *Gloster*, which had been enacted in the 6*th*. of that King's Reign.

(*a*) Stat. of Gloster 6. *E*. 1.

Some would think (*a*) those Statutes to have been no more than *Ordinances*, made by the *King* and his *Counsel* only: and that our Kings thus made *Ordinances* of that kind, some may gather from *Flet.*

(*b*) Habet Rex consil. suum in Parl. suis.

who speaks of the *King's Counsel* in which, not only erroneous Judgments were corrected, but new Remedies provided; yet *Flet.* speaks this of the *King's Counsel in his Parliaments*: and thus, tho

(*c*) Some Statutes made by the King, the Prelates, Earls, Barons, and his Council.

the Statute of *Westm*. 2. (*c*) seem to restrain the making that of *Gloster* to the *King* and his *Council* the Statute of *Gloster* it self shew that the *Counsel* was to be taken as acting in conjunction with the

Pr

of the Dependency of Ireland.

Prelates, Earls, and *Barons,* and that under the word *Barons* the Commonalty were included as is lower *Nobility,* or dignified by their Election to Parliament; accordingly the Statute of *Gloster* says suitably to latter Writs of Summons, the (a) *more discreet of the Kingd. as well Great as Small were Summon'd*: So that the Statutes of *Gloster* were made as other Statutes 3 *E.* 1. by that *King's Counsel,* and by *assent of the Commonalty;* where the *Lords* were manifestly included under the word (b, *Counsel,* agreeably to the ancient form of (c) Writs of *error,* or other Writs returnable into *Parliament, before us, and our Counsel in our Parliament, &c. at our next Parliament after, or at such a time, there to do what the King shall think fit to ordain, by advice of his Counsel.*

(a) 3. Inst. & Rot. Stat. de temp. E. 1. E. 2. E. 3. Appellez les plus discres de son regn, aussibien des greindres come des meindres. (b) per son consei', & per assentement des tout la Commonalty. (c) Vid. Regist. Brev. ed. An. 531. f. 17. Quod sint coram nobis & consilio nostro in Parl. nostro un. Rot. Claus. 17. E. 1. pars m. 8. Ad prox. Parl. post festum Paschæ, ut tunc inde Rex faciat quod de consilio suo duxerit ordinandum.

For evidence that this did not exclude the *Lords,* I may refer to the

The History and Reasons

the Rolls of *Parliament* of several Reigns, and particularly to those of the 20*th.* and 21*st.* of E. 3. In the 20*th.* the (*a*) Commons are desired to deliver such Petitions as were then ready, to the Clerk of the Parliament; which Petitions are said to be brought before the *Great Men of the Counsel.* That they were but of the nature of a *Committee* to inform the *King*, and *Lords*, of the *Bills* or *Petitions* which came from the *Commons*, appears by the Proceedings of the next Year; when the *Commons* having made *Petitions* of an extraordinary nature, the King answers, (*c*) " *He will advise with the Lords.* To return to the Statute of *Gloster*, there the *King* by such advice as I have shewn, made Laws for the amendment of *his Realm, and for the plenary exhibition of Right, as the profit of the Regal Office requires*; and to remedy (*d*) mischiefs, dammages, and disherisons, suffer'd by the *People of the Realm of* England; without the least mention of *Ireland.*

(*a*) Rot. Parl. 20. *E.*3. m. 11.

(*b*) Rot. Parl. 21, *E.*3 m.9. s'avisera ove les Grants.
(*c*) Rot. Stat. temps *E* 1.*E.*2. *E.* 3. Pur le amendment, de son Royaume & pour plenere exhibition de droit, si come le profit de office regal demand.
(*d*) Vid. the *Stat.* 3. *Inst.*

And

of the Dependency of Ireland.

And yet we have the judgment of the *Parliament* in the 13*th.* of that King, that *Ireland* was within the remedy of that *Statute,* as part of the *Realm of England,* as appears by this Preamble. (*a*) Where of "late our Lord the King in the "Quinzifme of St. *John Baptist,* the "Sixth of his Reign, calling toge- "ther the *Prelates, Earls, Barons,* "*and his Counsel*, at *Gloucester*; "and considering that divers *of* "*this Realm* were disherited by "reason that in many cafes where "remedy should have been had, "there was *none provided by him* "*nor his Predecessors*; ordained cer- "tain Statutes, right necessary "and profitable *for his People,* "*whereby the People of England,* "*and* Ireland *under his Government,* "*have obtained more speedy justice* "*in their oppressions than they had* "*before, and certain Cafes wherein* "*the Law failed* remain undeter- "mined, *and some remained to be* "*enacted,* that were for the reform "of the oppressions of *the People*; "Our Lord the King in *his Parlia-*
ment

(*a*) Weſt. 2. 13. E. 1. Anno 1285. Printed Stat.

(*b*) Stat. ed. An. 1529 Quædam ſtatuta populo ſuo valde neceſſaria utilia edidit, per quæ populus ſuus Anglicus & Hybernicus ſuo regimine gubernatus.

"ment, after the Feast of *Easter*, holden the 13th. of His Reign, at *Westminster*, caused many Oppressions of the *People* and defaults of the *Laws*, for the (c) supply of the defects of the said *Statutes* of Gloster, to be rehearsed and made Statutes, as will appear here following."

(c) Ad supletionem dict. Stat.

Et Statuta edidit.

This rehearsal of the Grievances was, for certain, by the *Petition* of the *Commons* of this Realm, and the Statutes there made, as the *Register* of Writs has it, were by the *Common Counsel of the Kingdom*: And this *Counsel* not only declared Laws which were binding to *Ireland*, but made new; tho' Mr. *Molineux* will have it, that from the time of *Magna Charta* to the 10th. of *H*. 7. no *Laws* were, or are in force in *Ireland*, unless allowed of by Parliament in that Kingdom: except only *such as are Declaratory of the Common Law of England, and not Introductive of any new Law.* And whereas he is pleas'd to say,

Vid. Regist. Writs f. 13. Quando uxor admittitur ad jus suum defendend. & f. 16. De communi consilio Regni nostri.

" As

of the Dependency of Ireland.   P. 81.

" As to such *English* Statutes as
" seem to comprehend *Ireland*,
" and to bind it *under the gene-*
" *ral words of all his Majesty's Do-*
" *minions, or Subjects*, whatever
" has been the opinion of private
" and particular Lawyers in this
" Point, *I am sure* (says he) *the*
" *Opinions of the Kings of* England,
" *and their Privy Council have*
" *been otherwise.* I may say upon
much better grounds, if any *King*
and His Privy *Council* did any thing
to Warrant this Assertion, the
Judgment of *E.* 1. and *His Coun-*
cil in *Parliament*, was to the contrary, and is of *greater Authority.*

And 'tis to be remembred, as
I before shewed, that the *Statutes*
of *Gloster*, which do not Name
Ireland, and the Statutes of *West.* 2.
which do, were both delivered to
the *Clerk* of the Justice of *Ireland,*
in order to their being published
and observed there. And 'tis
evident, that *Ireland*'s being bound
by *Parliaments* in *England*, without any consent expressed in *Ireland,* was not merely the Judgment

ment of the times above referred to, but the setled Judgment of that King and His *Council*, in His *Parliaments*.

Thus in (*a*) the 8*th* of that King, there's a Writ taking notice, that the *Irish* had desired to be governed by the Laws of *England*: upon which the *King* requires all the *English of the Land of* Ireland to Certifie, whether this might be granted without prejudice to them; declaring that the *King* would make *such Provision, as should seem expedient to Himself,* and *His Council*: which, plainly enough referred to His *Council in Parliament*. If, upon their Certificate, a general Law had passed to grant the *Irish* their Request, the mentioning the *consent* of the *English* there, could not be thought to derogate from the *Legislature* here; the Authority of which was intimated in that very reference, and was fully asserted in that *King's* Reign by an Act of Parliament, made here after that time, and the

(*a*) Priyn's Animad. on Lord Coke Pat. 8 *E*. 1. m. 13. Hib. Omnibus Anglicis terræ.

Quod nobis & consilio nstoro videbiturexpedire.

Proceedings

of the Dependency of Ireland.

ceedings thereupon, both in *England* and *Ireland*.

By the Case (*a*) of mixt Monies in *Ireland*, we are informed, that 29 *E*. 1. when, by the King's *sepecial Ordinance*, the *Pollards* and *Crochards* were cry'd down and made of no Value; the *same Ordinance was transmitted* into *Ireland, and Enrolled in the Exchequer* there, as is found in *the Red Book of the Exchequer* there.

(*a*)Davis Rep. f. 21. h. Issint 29 *E*. 1. quand per special ordinance del Roy, &c.

And agreeably to this, it appears by the Statute Roll here, that this *Ordinance*, which in truth was an Act of Parliament, or else an other of the same kind, was sent to *John Wogan*, then *Chief Justice* of *Ireland,* or to his Lieutenant.

Rot. Stat. de temp. *E*. 1. *E*. 2. *E*. 3. Johan Wogan, Justice Dirland, ou a son Lieutenant.

This is only a short Entry referring to the known usage; But the very next Record of a transmission to *Ireland* of a Statute made here, which was that about *Juries*, is more express.

Printed Stat. 21 *E*. 1. c. 1. Record 22 *E*. 1.

Mem.

Mem. quod istud Statutum de verbo ad verbum missum fuit in Hib. T. R. aput Kenynt. 14. die Aug. Rni sui 27. Et mandatum fuit J. Wogan Justic. Hib. quod præd. Stat. per totam Hib. in locis quibus expedire videret legi & publicè proclamari, & firmiter teneri faciat.

Mem. That that Statute, word for word, was sent into Ireland, *Teste the King at Kenynton* 14. *Aug. in the* 27th. *of his Reign. Command was given to* John Wogan, *Chief Justice of* Ireland, *to cause it to be read in those places in which he shall think it expedient, and to be publickly* Proclaimed *and* Observed.

Note a Stat. made in the 21 or 22 *was not sent to* Ireland *till the* 27th.

This Statute does not name *Ireland*, nor has general words which seem to include it: But it seems some years after to have been Enacted, that this Statute should be transcribed, and sent to *Ireland* for a Law given them by Parliamentary Authority.

In the 35th. of (a) *E. 1. Will. De Testa* was Impeach'd in *Parliament*, for grievous Oppressions and Extortions upon the People, by Colour of Authority from the *See of Rome*:

(a) Ryley's Placita Parl. f. 379. 381, 382.

pendency of Ireland.

, upon the Petition of
arons, and other *Great*
he *Commonality of the*
of England, occasio-
eral Law and Provi- *(a)* Pro Statu Coronæ Regiæ nec non terrarum ipsius Regis Scotiæ Walliæ & Hiberniæ.
State of the King's
also of His *Lands* of
les, and *Ireland*.
iedy was Enacted by
of the *King*, and the *b* Ex assensu Dom. Regis ac toto consilio Parliamenti.
il of Parliament; and
ed, that for the future
should not be permit-
(c) the *Realm*. *(c)* Non permitterentur in Regno.
and was then included
he *Realm*, appears not
intention before de-
agreeably thereunto,
then made is, by Et mandatum est Principi Walliæ & Com. Cest. & CustodiScotiæ & Justic. Hib.
of Parliament, sent to
of Ireland, as well as
of Governors of other
Dominions; enjoyning
nquire and proceed a-
who had offended in
id to cause the *Provision*, In eisdem terris firmiter & inviolabiliter observari.
and *Judgment*, of that
to be *Firmly* and In-
rved *in those Lands*.

Mr. *M.*

The History and Reasons

Ordinatio pro Statu Hib. falsly supposed to have been 17 E. 1.

P. 88.
Stat. ed An. 1529.

P. 88.

P. 89.

Vid. Rot. Clauf. 18. E. 1. m. 8.

Mr. *M*. having, as he thinks, answer'd an Objection from the *Ordinance for the State of* Ireland. Printed in our Statute-Books, not only that of 1670. but even in others much more Ancient, as made 17 *E.* 1. I shall shew him some new Matter, which may deserve his farther Consideration: and yet tho' he thinks he has prov'd, 1. That this *Ordinance* was never receiv'd in *Ireland*. 2. That 'twas *meerly an Ordinance* of the King, and *His Privy Council* in *England*; it might be enough to observe, That the Clause which he Instances in, forbidding the *King*'s Officers to purchase Lands there, upon pain of Forfeiture, has an *Exception for the King's Licence*; and tho' he has not been at the pains to examine whether there were any such Licences from *England*, I can shew him in the very next Year, a confirmation under the Great Seal of *England*, of a grant of *Land*'s there, before made from hence: which were sufficient security against the forfeiture.

ture. 2. If 'twere admitted that the Ordinance were made by the King and his *Privy Counsel*, 'twould be very difficult for him to prevail upon many to believe, that a *Land* or *Kingdom*, which in all the principal Parts of Government was under the controul of the Great Seal of another Kingdom, was (as he pretends) (a) *a complete Kingdom within it self*, (b) or *a Kingdom regulated within it self*; the contrary of which appears in numerous instances of the time of which we are at present enquiring; as of leave from hence to chuse Ecclesiastical Governors, Parsons, Directions, for the Proceedings of the *Courts* of *Justice*, and *Council* in *Ireland*; the appointing distinct *Courts* of *Judicature*, Grants of Lands, Offices, Liveries out of the King's Hands of Lands held in Chief of the Crown of *England*, Licences of alienation, and the like.

Further than all this, there's a Precedent of taxing *Communities* by Authority from hence. It must

Thes. & Bar. suis de ficcio Dublin. Pro Othone de Grandison.

(a) p. 148.
(b) p. 155.

I   be

be agreed, that 'twas frequent for *Kings* to grant to *Cities* and *Towns* in *England,* power to raise *Customs*, or *Duties* for *Murage*, the building or repairing their Walls, to be levyed upon Goods and Merchandizes brought thither; in these Grants there was no mention by what *advice*, or *consent* they issued; but 'tis to be presumed that the Great Seal was not rashly affixed; nor were they extended farther than to the Walls, which secured the Persons and Goods of those who paid the Duty: yet the *Great Seal of England* has been applyed much more absolutely, to the binding the property of the Subjects in *Ireland*, as may appear by this Record.

Pat. 18. E. 1. m. 13. De muragio Dublin.

R. Ballivis & probis hominibus suis Dublin Salutem Cum in subsidium villæ claudendæ vobis nuper per literas nostras Pat. concesserimus quod quasdam consuetudines usque ad certum tempus de sin-

The King to the Bayliffs and honest Men of Dublin Greeting; since, in aid of walling your Town, we lately by our Letters Patents granted, that you should take some Customs to a certain day, of every thing

to

gulis rebus venalibus ad eandem villam venientibus capietis, ac dilectus & Fidelis noster Nic. de Clere Thef. nost. Hibern. testificatus fuerit coram nobis, quod vos ad mandatum ejusd. Nic. magnam partem pecuniæ provende consuetud. antedict. in clausuram scaccar. nostri Dublin posuistis nos ea de causa, &c.

to be sold coming to that Town. And our beloved and faithful Subject Nic. de Clere Treasurer of Ireland has certified us, that you, at the command of the said Nicholas, have employed great part of the Money arising by those Customs, to the enclosing or repairing the Exchequer at Dublin. Therefore, &c.

The King by his Great Seal of *England* continues the Tax for Three Years longer than his first Grant, and allows of the applying part of it to an end very different from that of the *walling the Town*.

For a yet farther Evidence of the more absolute Dominion, which *E. 1.* exercis'd over *Ireland*, than he pretended to in *England*; I shall shew, that he took to himself Authority to set aside what is supposed to have been setled by an *Ordinance*, in the seventeenth of his Reign.

One of the said Ordinances provides, That neither *the Justice of Ireland, nor any other of the King's Officers, by colour of their Office, take Victuals from any Person without his Consent, unless in case of necessity,* and that by *the assent of the chief of the King's Council of those* Parts, and by Writ, out of the *Chancery of* Ireland.

<small>Ordin. pro Statu Hib. c. 2.</small>

And yet in the next Year after this *Ordinance* is supposed to have been made, the *King*, as a particular Indulgence to the *Citizens* of *Roscommon*, grants that the *Constable of Roscommon*, or other the King's Officers, shall take no *Victuals*, or other things of them without their Consent, *unless there be a necessity for it in time of War*. And this exemption is only by a Patent during *Pleasure*.

<small>Pat. 18 E. 1. M. 2.</small>

<small>Nisi tempore guerræ necessitas hoc deposcit.</small>

<small>Has literas nostras fieri fecimus patentes quamdiu nobis placuerit duratur'</small>

But, in truth, this was no violation of the *Ordinance* for the State of *Ireland*: For, besides that, I shall shew when 'twas made, and how, in another Reign; 'Tis certain it could

of the Dependency of Ireland.

could not be in a *Council* at *Nottingham* in the *Octaves* of St. *Martin*; not only as may appear to any one who will trace the Close and Patent-Rolls, and the Use of the Great Seal, which went along with the King from his Landing at *Dover* (a) on the 12th of *August*, to the (b) 16th of *November*; during which time the Seals were far from *Nottingham*, but chiefly because there was a *Parliament* at *Westminster*, appointed to be held on the *Crastino Martini*; which, 'tis to be presumed, met accordingly, tho' Mr. *M.* is positive that E. 1. 'c' held no *Parliament in the* 17th *of his Reign*.

But, for his Conviction in this particular, during *d* the K's Absence in Foreign Parts, *Edmund* Earl of *Cornwall*, being *Custos*, Dated the Writs, among which there was one referring a Matter to the Judgment of the King and his Council, in the *next Parliament to be after* Easter.

And to satisfie Mr. *M.* that there was no need of a *Council at Nottingham*

(a) Clauf. 17. E. 1. M. 4. Intus. Nota Oct. Martini, *is but* 2 *Days after.*

(b) P. 89.

(c) Clauf. 17. E. 1. M. 8. Utque ad proximum Parl. post Pascha ut tunc inde Rex faciat quod de concilio suo duxerit ordinandum. Teste Edm. Com. Corn. Conf. Regis apud. West. 5 Martii.

ham, nor could there be one the *Octaves* of St. *Martin*, it happens that on (*a*) the 14th of that *October*, a Writ issued to the *Sheriff* of *Nottingham*, acquainting him of a Commission to certain Persons to hear the Miscarriages of the King's Officers in that Country, and to give me an account thereof at the *next Parliament* ; and therefore commands the *Sheriff* to Summon all Parties aggrieved, to be at *Westminster* that year in the Morrow of *Sanct* (*b*) *Martin*.

I must own that I have not found any Record of a *Writ of Summons* for any of the Members to come to Parliament that Year, nor has Sir *William* (*a*) *Dugdale* found any to the *Lords*, till the 22d ; and yet 'twill be agreed, that there were Parliaments between the 49th of *H*. 3. and the 22d of *E*. 1. and 'tis certain the Statute of *Westm*. 1. (*b*) 3 *E*. 1. is express, that the *Archbishops*, *Bishops*, *Abbots*, *Priors*, *Earls*, *Barons*, and *all the Commonalty of the Land*, were Summoned to that *General Parliament*,

---

(*a*) Claus. 17. *E*. 1. M. 2. dorso Nobis ea in proxim. Parl. nostro referant

(*b*) Quod veniant apud Westm. in Crast. instantis Festi Sancti Martini.

That 'tis to be believed a Parliament was holden 17 *E*. 1. *tho no Summons to it found.*

(*a*) Vid. Dugdale's *Summons to the Nobility. That which he cites* 5 *E*. 1. *is a Summons to the Army.*

(*b*) Vid. Stat. ed. An. 1529. p. 21.

of the Dependency of Ireland.

ment, and *assenting to the Laws then made.*

Mr. *Prynn*, as I take it, had not seen any Writ of *Summons* to the *Commons,* till 26 *E.* 1. Yet I have found in the Close-Roll of (a) 18 *E.* 1. as Dr. *Brady,* and Mr. *Petyt* have in the Bundle of *Writs,* this following.

Of A Summons to Parliament 18 *E.* 1.

(a) Rot. Clauſ. 18. *E.* I. M. 10. dorſo.

Rex. Vic. Northumb: cum per Com. Bar. & quoſdam alios de proceribus regni noſtri, nuper fuiſſemus requiſiti ſuper quibuſdam tam cum ipſis quam cum aliis de comitatibus regni illius, colloquium habere velimus & tractatum; Tibi præcipimus, quod duos vel tres de diſcretioribus & ad laborandum potentioribus militibus, de Com. præd. eligi & eos ad nos uſq; Weſtm. venire facias ; fine	The King to the Sheriff of Northumberland. *Forasmuch as we were lately in a special manner entreated by the* Earls, Barons, *and some others of the* Peers, *or* Nobility *of our* Realm, *that we would have a* Colloquy *and* Treaty *upon some Matters*, as well with them, as with others *of the* Counties of *the* Realm. *We require you without delay, to cause to be Elected, and to come to us as far as* Westminster, two or three of the more	That cit d by Dr. Brady *is to the Sheriff of* Weſtmorland.

dilatione. Ita quòd sint ibid. à die Sancti ibidem a die Sancti Johannis Baptistæ prox. fatur in tres septimanas ad ultimum, cum plenâ potestate pro se & totâ Communitate comitat. præd. ad consulendum & consentiendum pro se & communitat. illâ, hiis quæ Com. Bar. & Proceres præd tum duxerint concordand. T. R. apud West. 14 die Junii.

more discreet, and more able to travail of the Knights of *the said* County: *So that they be there at the latest, within* three Weeks, *from the Day of St.* John *the Baptist next ensuing, with* full power *for themselves, and* all the Commonalty of the said County, to consult and consent *to those things, which the aforesaid* Earls *and* Barons *shall then think fit to be agreed. Test. the King at* Westm. *the* 14th *day of* June.

Dr. *Bradie's* Answ. p. 230. Dr. *Bradie's Introduction to his Compleat History.*

This Dr. *Brady*, in his Answer to Mr. *Petyt*, more truly than he is aware, calls a *Summons* to a *Parliament*: However in his Introduction he will have it, that the Laws were then made by *the King* and his *Peers*, before the *Knights* of the *Shires* came; the Statute of that time saying, that the *Parliament* was

of the Dependency of Ireland.

was holden in the *Quinzism* of St. *John*, and that the Laws were made at the (a) *Instance* of the *Great Men*.

But he might have observed,

1. That the Provision (b) then made, is called a *Statute*.
2. That the *Council* wherein it pass'd, is called a *Parliament*.
3. That the Matter enacted, was a *general Law*, and of *general Concern*; it being for the encouraging of Purchasers, and engaging the more Persons to a National Interest by Propriety in Land, which till that time was in much fewer Hands; because whoever purchased any part of an Estate, had been liable to be charged with all the Rents and Services which lay upon the whole; and there was one other necessary Provision, against Alienations in *Mortmain*.
4. The Precept to the *Sheriff* was to cause the Election to be made *forthwith*, and to take care that the Parties were *found* to be at *Westminster* by three Weeks after the Feast of St. *John*, at the farthest.

(a) Ad instantiam Magnatum.

(b) Et sciendnm est quod istud statutum tenet locum de terris venditis tenend. in feodo simpliciter tantum. Quia emptores terrar. &c. There us'd to be Manucaptors for this purpose.

theft. The Day when the *Parliament* was holden, was but 5 or 6 Days before; which shews, that 'tis absurd to imagine, that there should have been a Law made of that immediate consequence to all Owners of Land, before the *Knights* of the *Shire* came up; not only because they being obliged to be at *Parliament* by such a Day *at the latest*, may well be supposed to have come 5 or 6 Days before the utmost extent of their time, to avoid the Forfeitures of the Bonds, which they us'd to give for their Appearance; but chiefly, because, as 'tis well known, whenever a Law passes, 'tis in Judgment of Law held to have pass'd the first Day of the *Session*; which Day might have been agreed at their former Meeting. Nor is it absurd to believe, that there might be a *Summons* to require the *Sheriffs* to secure *Full Parliaments*, even tho the Days of Meeting and of Elections below, might have been certain.

The

of the Dependency of Ireland.

The true reason why so few Writs of Summons, of those early times, are to be found, seems to be, that once, at least, in a Year the *Parliaments* met of course. *Why so few Writs of Summons in those Times now to be found.*

The *Confessor's* Law speaks of the (a) *Calends of May* as the fix'd Day. In the (b) 1st of *E* 1. the *Custos* of the *Realm*, as appears above, in the King's Absence issued Writs, who not for Elections to *Parliament*, yet returnable into the *Parliament*, to be holden next *after Easter*, without mentioning any Day, as if 'twere commonly known; but no Parliament being holden soon after *Easter*, because of the King's being out of the Land, a Return into a *Parliament* appointed to sit after the King's Landing, was to a Day certain. But that at the beginning of *E.* 1. the time of holding a *Parliament* was look'd upon as so fix'd, that there was no need of *Summons*, appears by that *King's* Letter to the *Pope*, 3 *E.* 1. referring him to the Deliberation of the *Peers* of the Kingdom in a *Parliament*,

(a) Vid. *Lamb's Archaionom Leges* St. *Edw.*
(b) Rot. Claus. 17. *E.*1. sup.

Rot. Claus 3. *E.*1. *M.*9. dorso in Parl. Quod circa octabas Resurrectionis Domini celebrari in Angliâ consuevit.

ment, which used to be holden in England, *about the Octaves of the Resurrection of our Lord.*

5. If the mention only of the *Instance* of the Great Men, or *Nobility*, be an Argument that the Law was then made before even the *Knights* of the Counties came up, tho Summoned to *Consult* and *Consent* ; the many Laws which have pass'd immediately upon the *King*'s Answer to the *Petition* of the *Commons*, would argue as strongly, that those Laws were made without the consent of *the Lords* ; but as in such case, either they were included as part of the *Community* of the *Kingdom*, or else the *King* answered *by their Advice* ; So at the making the *Statute* 18 *E*. 1. either the *Commons* were under the Word *Magnates*, as the *lower Nobility*, or Men dignified by being Senators, or else the *Great Lords* finding themselves chiefly agrieved, as being unable to pay their Debts, because none would buy their Lands; this Law might have pass'd chiefly at their desire : But then, since 'tis mani-

of the Dependency of Ireland.

manifest it was in P*arliament*,'twas by the Consent of the *Commons*; but I rather think that the *Commons* were then included under *Magnates*, because I find them so in Times after this; and that Petitions were made to them with as *high Ascriptions* as were given to the *Great Lords*.

Commons included under Magnates.

In the 1st of *E. 3.* a Statute was made, as one Record has it, by the (*a*) *Common Council* of the *Kingdom*, as another (*b*) by the *King*, the *Prelates, Earls, Barons, and the Commonalty of the Realm*; and yet an Historian well conversant in the Records, and common acceptation of Words in that Time, speaking of this very P*arliament*, and of the Queen Mother's coming to *London*, with *E. 3.* her Son, says, *Thither also Convened the* whole (*c*)Nobility *of the* Kingdom, *having been before Summoned to the* holding a Parliament.

(*a*) Rot. Pat. 1 E.3. M. 10.
(*b*) Rot. Claus. 2 E.3. M. 20.

Walsingham, F. 126.

(*c*)Tota regni nobilitas citata per prius ad Parl. semend.

In after Times there are numbers of Petitions to the *House of Commons*, from Persons of Quality; from the City of *London*, and others:

The History and Reasons

(b) Rot. Clauf. 4. H. 4. n. 19. Pur Monsieur Thomas Pomercy Chivalier. Tres honourables & Tressages Communes.
(e) Rot. Parl. 8. H. 6. n. 51. Tressages & Tres honourables.
From the Mayor, Aldermen and Commons of the City of London. Rot. Patl. 3. H. 5. pars 1. n. 7 Vid. Sup. of Cities and Boroughs.

thers: To *the (a)* Most Honourable, *or* Right Honourable, *and* Most Wise *the* Commons in this present Parliament Assembled.

The *(b) Honourable* and *Most wise,* and the like.

(c) But some who will admit that the *Knights* of the Shire, who indeed are in many Records call'd *Grands* of the *Counties,* were part of the *Magnates* 17 E. 3. will have it, that the *Citizens* and *Burgesses* were not, because. 1. They, in those Times, used to be distinguished by the Name of *Commons,* from the Knights of the *Shires.* 2. There's no mention of any *Summons* to them in the Records of 18 E. 1. when there was to the *Knights* of the *Shires.* But for a full answer to this, I desire it may be considered.

Vide sup.

1. That the Meeting 17 E. 1. appears by the Statute then made, to be a *Parliament,* that Dr. *Brady* himself has yielded, that the *Cities, Boroughs,* and *Cinque Ports,* and *Vills,* had by King *John's Charter,* right to be of the *Common-Counci*

of the Dependency of Ireland.

Council of the Kingdom; which is the Phrase most generally used in the Ancient *Register of Writs,* to denote a *Parliament.*

2. There were *Boroughs* long before the reputed *Conquest*: As for instance, St. *Edmund's Bury,* or *Burgh,* made a Borough in the Time of King *Edmund,* confirmed in the Reigns of *Cnute,* the *Confessor, W.* 1. and other Kings.

3. *Boroughs* frequently occur in *Dooms-day Book,* that great Survey taken in the Reign of *W.* 1. and are mentioned as such in the Time of *Edward the Confessor.*

4. No one *Charter* of ancient Times since *W.* 1. can be found, giving any *Borough* right to send Members to *Parliament*; but that has seem'd the consequent of being a *Borough,* having a *Gild* for Merchandize, and answering to the King, or other chief Lord, as one entire Body: upon which account they appeared by Representation, while individual *Tenants* were in the great *Councils* upon their Personal Right.

5. That

5. That for asserting the Right of *Boroughs* to be represented in Parliament, it generally was enough to plead that they were *Boroughs*; yet one instance at least is to be found within two Reigns after the time of our present enquiry, where a (*a*) *Borough* Pleads, or Alledges in P*arliament*, that they had been made a *Borough* in King *Athelstan*'s time, and ever after had been represented in P*arliament* by two Members of their own chusing: and this the then P*arliament*, or the *King's Council* in it, were so far from thinking improbable, that upon that Borough's Allegation that the Charter was lost, they direct an enquiry, with declared disposition to have it renewed.

(*a*) Rot. Pat. 17. E. 3. p. 1. m. 20. dorso.

6. These *Boroughs*, whether holding of the *Crown* in chief, or of *Great Lords*, were either *Baronies*, or parts of *Baronies*, upon the account of *Knights Service*; or *Honors* by

of the dependency of Ireland.

by reason of other free Tenures, and their Charters, that they should hold *freely* and *honourably*, as many of them run; and thus the Members in P*arliament*, who serv'd for these *Baronies*, or *Honours*, were part of the *Baronage* of the Kingdom: Not but that sometimes *Barony* and *Honour* are used without distinction concerning them; and thus that ancient Borough of *Barnstaple* (a) which held of the Lord *Tracy*, is in the same Record call'd both a *Barony*, and an *Honour*. Which Honour, as appears by this instance, was not limited to immediate Tenure of the Crown; and that this was not derived from the grant of a reputed *Conqueror* might be proved by numbers of Authorities, of which I shall here content my self with one out (a) of *Doomesday-Book*.

Libere & honorifice.

(a) Pat. 15. Jo. parf. 1. M. 11 Reddidimus Hen. de Tracy Baroniam de Bardeftaple. Ib. Dotum honorem de Bardeftaple.

(a) Vid. *Doomsday* de Norwic.

In Norwic erant temp. E. MCCCXX Burgenses, &c. Tota hæc villa redde-	*In* Norwich *there were in the time of* Edward 1320. *Burgesses. All this*
K	bat

bat TRE 20 l. Regi & Comiti 10 l. In novo Burgo (*a*) XXXVI Burgenses and VI Anglici. De hoc toto habebat Rex 2 partes & Comes tertiam; modo XLI Burgenses Franci in dominio Regis, & Comes Rogerus Bigot habet L. & sic de aliis. Tota hæc terra Burgensium erat in Dominio Comitis Rad. & concessit eam Regi in commune, ad faciendum Burgum inter se & Regem : Ut testatur Vicecomes.

(*a*) Nota, What a small proportion this new Plantation of French bore to the 1320 Burgesses, and yet some English were mix'd even among the French. Besides the French seem to have had but 11 added to their number from the Confessors time to the 20th. of W. 1.

Town in the time of King Edward yielded the King 20 l. and the Earl 10 l. In the new Borough there were 36 Burgesses, and six of them English. Of all this the King had two parts, and the Earl the third. Now there are 41 Burgesses in the Kings demeasn, and Earl Roger Bigot has 50. and so of others. All this Land of the Burgesses was in Earl (*c*) Ralphs Demeasn, and he granted it to the King in common, to make a Borough between him and the King: As the Sheriff attests.

This Earl was *Ralph Guader* or *Wader*, who continued Earl of *Norfolk*, or at least of *Norwich*, from

of the Dependency of Ireland.

from within the *Confessor*'s Reign, till the 9*th.* or 10*th.* of *W.* 1.

7. The Freemen, or at least they who had Borough-holds in these, or in some of them, are in *Doomsday-Book,* called *Barons,* as particularly in the *Borough* of *Warwick.*

| Et in Burgo de Warwic habet Rex in Dominio suo CXIII Domus, & Barones Regis habent CXII. de quibus omnibus Rex habet geldam. | *And in the Borough of* Warwick *the King has in his demeasm* 113 *Houses, and the Kings Barons have* 112. *of all which the King has Aid.* |

8. They who were interested in the Government of these *Boroughs,* and had Right to look after their common concerns, could not but be *Barons* as properly, as the Free hold Tenants of *Lords* of *Mannors, Freeholders,* who were Judges in the County Courts, and the *Freemen* of *London,* who are call'd Barons in several Records, and
other

other undoubted Authorities, and the *Barons* of the Cinque Ports.

(*a*) *Doomſday-Book* TRE reddebat, &c.

Of *Dover* in particular (*a*) *Doomſday Book* ſays, in the time of *King Edward* it yielded 18 *l.* of which *King Edward* had two parts, and *Earl Godwin* the 3. And a *Charter*(*c*) to this *Port* in the beginning of *King John's* Reign confirms to his Men of *Doura* the *Confeſſor's* Charter, together with the Charters of *W.* 1. and other Kings after the reputed Conqueſt.

(*b*) Rot. Cart. 2. Jo. m. 17. n. 51.

9. If 'tis to be thought, that no *Citizens* and *Burgeſſes* were at the Parliament 17 *E.* 1. becauſe no Summons appears for other *Commons,* beſides the Knights of the *Shires* ; by the ſame reaſon 'tis to be thought, that none of the *Great Lords* were there ; no *Summons* to them appearing.

10. In

of the Dependency of Ireland.   149

10. In the Writs for chusing Knights of the Shires there was no occasion to mention the choice of others; and thus 12 *E.* 2. Only the *Earls, Barons,* and *Commonalty* of the Counties are spoken of as granting an 18*th.* part of their Goods: but they would be very much deceiv'd who should think, that no others were at that Parliament; for the same Record shews, that the *Clergy* granted a 10*th.* and the *Cities* and *Boroughs* a 12*th.*   Rot. Pat. 12. *E.* 2. m. 5.

11. 'Tis very probable that at that time, the *Cities* and *Boroughs* had the Writs directed to them in particular, to be return'd by their *Headborough,* or other Officer, or else by the Community there.

Thus in the 14*th.* of King *John* a Summons to the Army is sent to the *Headborough* and *Honest Men* of *Canterbury*; so to *Dover, Rochester, Gildford,* and a great many other Places.   Rot. Claus. 14. Jo. m. 8. d.

K 3   And

And the very next Year particular Writs are sent to the *Honest Men* of *Canterbury*, the *Mayor* and *Barons* of *London*, the *Mayor* and *Honest Men* of *Winchester*, &c. and so to all the *Boroughs* and Demesns of the Crown; not only referring them to the *Justice* or *Custos* of the Realm, but desiring an Aid of them which: Mr. *M.* must agree to have been desired in as true a *Parliamentary Meeting*, as those which he cites of the time of *H.*3. in relation to *Ireland*.

<small>Rot. Pat. 15. Jo. m. 3. n. 8.</small>

This I hope may not be thought an unprofitable digression from the supposed *Ordinance* 17 *E.* 1. but may sufficiently evince, by what Authority it must have been made, if there were any such of that time; and that the King and his *Counsel* pretended not to settle the State of a Dominion annex'd to the Crown of *England*, without consent of the States.

But

of the Dependency of Ireland.   151

But tho' the *King's Counsel* did not then act in *Parliament matters*, otherwise than *Parliamentarily*; yet 'tis certain that they did exercise an *Ordinary Jurisdiction* in relation to *Ireland*, as well as to *England*, either as *Committees* or Tryers of Petitions, appointed by the Lords or otherwise; tho' the bringing a Cause from the Lords in *Ireland to the House of Lords* here, is one of the circumstances in *the present juncture of Affairs, which seems to require Mr.* M's *learned Disquisition*.

In the Bundle of Petitions to the Parliament, in the time of *E.* 1. there are some (*a*) endorsed as brought before the *King*, some before *all the Council*; and as the Method of following times explains this Matter, there had been appointed Receivers and Tryers of Petitions concerning *Ireland*; for several are receiv'd from thence, and authoritatively Answered.

Bundela Pet. Parl. de temp. *E.* 1.
(*a*) Coram toto consilio.

There's

There's one from *Jeffery de Geymul*, who complains of the *Barons* of the *Exchequer* in *Ireland*, for sending within his Jurisdiction, a Commission of enquiry, who Sold *Pollards*; to the prejudice, as he alledged, of the *Franchise*, which (a) *H. 2.* had granted to the Ancestors of his Wife, *Maud de Lacy*.

(a) Vid. Davis Rep. le case del County Pal. f. 64. Carr. *H. 2.* Hugoni de Lacy Com. pro serv. suo & terram in Midea cum omnibus pertin' per serv. 50. militum sibi & hær. suis tenend. de me & hær. meis.

This Commission was manifestly founded upon the Record of the Statute made here, as is shewn above, enrolled in the *Exchequer* of *Ireland* by Order from hence: This the *Barons* there obey'd, and held that by Virtue of that, they might cause Commissions of Enquiry to be executed even in *Palatinates*: nor does it appear, that the *King's Council* in *Parliament* disallowed of their Proceedings; for nothing was done upon this *Petition*, any more than referring it to the next *Parliament*.

In

of the Dependency of Ireland.

In the Case of one *Allen Fitzwaren*, they Ordered a Writ from the *Chancellor of England*, to require the *Justice of Ireland* to examine, whether a Judgment about Title of Land had been given while a Man was absent, and under the *King's Protection*; requiring, that *if any thing was done contrary to Protection, it should be amended in due manner.*

And as the *Lords* in *Parliament* then exercis'd a Jurisdiction over *Ireland*; it appears that out of it the *High Admiral of England* had Conusance, of all *maritime Causes*, as well throughout *Ireland*, as *England*, from the time then beyond the memory of Man, which must relate to the general Prescription, which is at this day as far since as the beginning of *R. 1.* Son to *H. 2.*

Rot. de superioritate Maris 26. *E.* 1. Les Roys du dit Royaume du temps dount il n'a memore du contraire eussent este en paisible poss. de la Soveraign Seignorie, de la meer Dengleterre, & des Isles avec la conusteants en y cel & q. l'Admiral ad jurisd. nuisance & justice & touts autres appertenants, *&c.*

That

That during the Reign of *E.1.Irel.* was govern'd as a part of *England*, or appurtenant to it; and that the Laws made here wanted no other Publication, than what was in obedience to the Great Seal of *England*, affixed to Writs and Charters, or Exemplifications of our Acts of Parliament, by Authority from hence, I think may be beyond dispute: which might excuse my not dwelling upon the unfortunate Reign of *E.* 2. and yet there are some evidences not to be neglected of *England*'s being then possess'd of its ancient Authority over *Ireland*: and that, tho' at least from the 3*d.* of that King's Reign Mr. *M.* supposes, that they had *a regular Legiflature* in *Ireland.*

*Of Ireland's being bound by the Parliaments of England in the time of E.*2.

In the 10*th.* of that King, the *English* in *Ireland* petitioned him for a Constitution, that a *Parliament* should be holden there once a Year; Upon this and other things then desired, the King, under the Great Seal

Prynn'*s* Animad. on Lord Coke f. 262. 10. *E.*2. Quod semel in Anno teneatur Parl.

Seal of *England*, commands the *Justice* of *Ireland* to Summon a *Parliament* there, to consider what was fit to be done, and to certifie the result into *England*: upon which the *King* declared that he would, by the *advice of* his *Counsel*, ordain what should be fitting: but nothing more appears of that matter, which was the farthest step towards settling an *Annual Parliament* in *Ireland*.

In the 12*th.* of that *King* an Act of *Parliament* was made in *England*, with this Preamble, "Forasmuch "as divers People of the Realm " of *England*, and of the Land " of *Ireland*, have heretofore ma- " ny times suffered great Mischiefs, " Damage, and Disherisons, by " reason that in some Cases *where* " *the Law failed, no Remedy was* " *ordained*; and also forasmuch as " some points of the Statutes here- " tofore made, had need of Ex- " position; *our Lord King* Edward, " *Son to King* Edward, desiring " that full Right may be done to "*his*

Stat. of York 12 E. 2.

"his People; at his Parliament hol-
"den at *York*, the third Week af-
"ter the Feaft of St. *Michael*, the
"12th Year of his Reign by the
"*Affent* of the *Prelates*, *Earls*,
"*Barons*, and the *Commonalty* of
"his *Realm* there affembled, hath
"made thefe *Acts* and *Statutes*
"following; the which he wil-
"leth to be obferv'd in his faid
"*Realm*, and *Land*.

Though *Ireland* is in fome fenfe part of the *Realm* of *England*, yet here 'tis diftinguifhed as a *Land* intended to be bound, tho it had no *Commonalty* of its own to reprefent it in *Parliament*: and there is *new Remedy provided where the Law has failed*, as well as the explaining what was Law before: that part at leaft which creates a Forfeiture of *Wine* and *Victuals* fold by any Officer appointed to look after the Affifes of them, was abfolutely new.

Cap. 6.

This

of the Dependency of Ireland. 157

This Statute was transmitted to *Ireland*, by the following Writ, under the *Great Seal* of *England*, and the Name of the Party who received it, is enter'd upon Record.

Rot. Sat. de temp. E.1.E.2. E.3. Statuta missa fuerunt in Hib. ut in brevi subseq. continetur, & liberata fuerunt Godf. filio Rog. una cum dict. brev. deferend.

Rex Cancel. suo Hibern' Salutem. Quædam statuta per nos in Parl. no-ro nuper apud Ebor'convocato, de assensu Prel. Com. &r. & totius Communitatis, regni nostri ibid' existen- ; ad Commun. util. regni nostri terræ Hibern' e-a, vobis sub sigillo nostro mittimus insignata. Man-ntes quod Stat. in dicta Cancel iâ custodiri, ac in rotulis ejusd. Cancel. irrotulari, & sigillo nostro quo utimur in Hi-

The King to his Chancell. of Ireland, *Greeting, We send you under our* Great Seal, *certain* Statutes *made* by us *in* our Parliament lately called together at *York, with the* Assent *of the* Prelates, Earls, Barons, *and* all the Commons of our Kingdom there assembled ; *for the* Common Utility *of* our Kingdom, *and* Land *of* Ireland : *Commanding you, that those* Statutes be kept in the Rolls of the said Chancery, to be enroll'd and berniâ in forma patenti exemplificari, & ad singulas placeas nostras in ter.præd. & singulos comitat. ejusd. ter.mitti facias, & brevia nostra sub dicto sigillo minist. nostris placearum illar. & Vicecom. dict. Com. quod statuta illa coram ipsis publicari & ea in omnibus & singulis suis artic. quantum ad eor. singulos pertinet, firmiter faciant observari. Teste R. apud Clarendon 10 die Sept. An.quarto decimo.

and exemplified in the Form of a Patent under our Seal which we use in *Ireland: and that you cause it to be sent to every one of our Places in the said Land, and every County of the same. And our Writs under our said Seal, commanding our Officers of those Places, and Sheriffs of the said Counties, to cause those Statutes to be* published *before them, and in all and singular their Articles which to every one of them appertain, to be* firmly observ'd. Teste *the* King *at* Clarendon *the 10th of* Sept. *in the 14th of his Reign.*

In the same Roll there's another Writ of the same Form, dated at
Not

of the Dependency of Ireland.

Nottingham 20 *Nov.* sending to the Chancellor of *Ireland,* the Stature of *York,* and another made before at *Lincoln.*

These Entries explain the general Transmissions; and shew what was to be done by the *Justice of Ireland,* in order to the publication of Laws made in P*arliaments* here, and sent to him: but yet he had no need nor authority to call a *Parliament in Ireland,* for the publishing any Law made here, unless particularly required under the Great Seal of *England.*

Yet I cannot but admire the force of Mr. *M*'s Imagination, in framing an Argument, on that very Year that those Statutes were sent to *Ireland,* That the P*arliament of* England *did not take upon them to have any jurisdiction in* Ireland, because the King sent his Letters-Patents to the Lord Chief Justice of *Ireland,* commanding that the *Irish* Natives might enjoy the *Laws of* England concerning Life and Member; to which *he had been moved*

Pag. 130.
Pag. 129.

The History and Reasons

moved by his Parliament *at* Westminster: which is as much as to say, they used no Jurisdiction because they did.

That after this time, that *King* and his *Parliament* exercised Jurisdiction over *Ireland*, appears by the *Ordinance* made for the State of *Ireland*, in a Parliament held on the *Octaves* of St. *Martin*, in the 17th of his Reign, and not of *E.* 1. for which I shall refer not only to what I before observed, which may give reasonable satisfaction that no such *Ordinance* could have been made in the 17th of *E.* 1. but to the Statute-Rolls, where this is entered among the Statutes of the time of *E.* 2. next above the Statutes of the time of *E.* 3. For maintaining the Jurisdiction of *England* that Statute of *Nottingham* ordains, "That no Pardon for Felony be granted by the Justice of *Ireland*, nor Seal'd with the King's Seal there, *without special Command of the King, under some one of his Seals of* England.

Rot. Stat. temp. E. 1. E. 2. E. 3. M. 30.

1. It

of the Dependency of Ireland.

1. It being so manifest from undoubted Records, that the Parliaments of *England*, to the 17th. of *E.* 2. exercised an Authority in making *Laws* to bind *Ireland*, and that there was a plain and known Method for publishing those Laws in *Ireland* by virtue of the Great Seal of *England*, I hope it will be allowed, that the Authority of Sir *Richard Bolton*'s Marginal Note in an Edition of the *Irish Statutes*, is not enough to induce Men to believe, that in the 13th. of *E.* 2. the Statute of *Merton*, 20th. *H.* 3. and some other Statutes made in *England*, were confirmed in *Ireland*, as being of no force there till then: And that no other Statutes made in *England* were of force in *Ireland*, till confirm'd there. Can any Man think that no part of the Statute of *Merton* was received for Law in *Ireland* till the 13th. of *E.* 2. particularly, will even Mr. *M.* believe, that notwithstanding the Record 21. *H.* 3. of Transmission of so much at least of the Statute of *Merton* as relates to the *Limitation of Writs*, yet till the 13th. of *E.* 2. the descent in a

Answer to Sir Richard Bolton's Marginal Note.

P. 63. 64.

Vid. Sup.

L   Writ

Writ of Right was to be lay'd from an Ancestor of the time of *H.* 1. which is 200 Years within One? Or does he think that the *Justice* of *Ireland*, for the time being, would not have been turn'd out, if not impeached, had he not caused the *Statutes of West.* 1. and 2. and the *Statutes* of *Gloucester*, to have been *Proclaimed* and *Observed* in *Ireland*, after they had been delivered to his Clerk in the Parliament at *Winchester?* and yet, if there be any thing in Mr. *M*'s Quotation from Sir *Richard Bolton*, these were not received for *Laws* in *Ireland* till 13. *E.* 2.

But since 'tis manifest that those, and the other Statutes afterwards sent over in the time of *E.* 1. and *E.* 2. must needs have been put in Execution there; if there were any such Act of *Parliament* 13. *E.* 2. as Mr. *M.* takes for granted, upon no Authority in comparison with the Records which I have cited; as to so much of any Acts of *Parliament* made here, as was not transmitted in the form above shewn, the Enacting them in *Ireland* might be the first *Publication*

Stat. Merton c. 7. De Narratione in brevi de recto ab antecessore a tempore Hen. Regis senioris.

Vid. Sup.

of the Dependency of Ireland.

tion there: But as to what was contained in the *Patent* or *Charter* sent thither, it could be no more than a *Declaratory Law*, or rather *Republication*.

Sometimes there might have been a special form of Transmission, which as one means of publishing the Laws, might require their *Parliament* to meet to hear Laws read to them, which would bind them whether they consented or no: or by Writ from hence, a Law or Charter pass'd there might be so republished. Thus 'twas beyond Contradiction 12. H. 3. when a Charter of King *John's*, sworn to by the *Irish*, was either sent back, or republished after it had lain there.

Mr. *M.* p. 52. and 53. *Rot. Clauf.* 12. H. 3. *De legibus & conf. observandis in Hib.*

Rex dilecto & fideli suo Ric. de Burgo Justic. suo Mandamus vobis firmiter, præcipientes quatenus certo die & loco faciatis venire coram vobis Arch. Ep. Ab. Pr. Com. & Bar. Mil. & libere tenentes, & Bal-

The King to his Beloved and Faithful Subject Richard de Burgh, *his Justice of* Ireland, *we command you, firmly requiring, that at a certain day and place, you cause to come before you the Arch-Bishops, Bishops, Abbots, Priors, Earls, & Barons, Knights, &*

L 2 *Free-*

livos singulor. Co-
mitat. & coram eis
publice legi faciatis
cartam Dni. J.Regis
Patris nri cui Sigil-
lum sum appensum
est quam fieri fecit
& jurari à Magnati-
bus Hib. de legibus
& consuetud. Ang-
licis observandis : &
præcipiatis exparte
nostrâ quod leges,
illas & consuetudi-
nes in carta præd.
contentas de cætero
firmiter teneant. Et
hoc idem per singu-
los Comitatus Hib.
clamari faciatis &
teneri, Prohibentes
firmiter exparte no-
strâ, & super foris-
factur. nostram ne
quis contra hoc Man-
datum venire pre-
sumat.

Freeholders, and the Bailiffs of every County: and before them cause publickly to be read the Charter of King *John our Father, to which his Seal is affixed, which he caused to be made and sworn by the great Men of* Ireland; *concerning the observing in* Ireland *the Laws and Customs of* England. *And command them from us, that they, for the future, firmly keep and observe the Laws and Customs in the said Charter contained. And cause this same to be Proclaimed thro' every County of* Ireland, *firmly Prohibiting in our Name, and under our Forfeiture, that no person presume to the contrary of this our Command.*

All must agree that this Publication, in so formal a *Parliament*, and after

of the Dependency of Ireland.

after that, in the several *Counties*, was not necessary to give Sanction to that Charter, for that it had before: And could be no more than a reminding them of their Duty, or a more solemn *Publication* of the *Law*. But that being a Law made here, was held sufficient to make it a Law to the *English* in *Ireland*, and that, being transmitted thither under the Great Seal of *England*, it became a Rule to the Judges there, even in matters happening before the transmission, appears by the following Precedents. Rot. Claus. 20. H. 3. m. 13.

A Man having been redisseis'd after the Statute of *Merton*, 20. H. 3. which had made a Redisseisour lyable to Imprisonment. A Party, who had been so injured, applies to the King for Remedy, and as the Writ to the Justice of *Ireland* has it,

Ideo vobis mittimus sub sigillo nostro constitutionem nuper factam coram nobis & Magnatibus nostris Angliæ, de prædicto casu & si-	*Therefore we send you, under our Seal, the Constitution, lately made before us and our great Men of* England, *concerning that Case, and other Ar-*

militer, de aliis articulis ad emendationem rni nri Mandantes quat. de *consilio* venererab. Pat. L. Dublin, Arch. constitutionem illam in Curiâ noſtra Hib. legi & de cætero firmiter obſervari, faciatis, & ſecund. eandem præd. querenti plene juſtitiam exhiberi faciatis.

Articles, for the Amendment of this our Kingdom, commanding, That with the Counſel of the venerable father L. Arch-Biſhop of Dublin, *you cauſe that Conſtitution to be read in our Court of* Ireland, *and for the future to be firmly obſerved, and that you fully do juſtice to the Complainant according to the ſame.*

In the Senſe, in which the Parliament 12. of *H.* 3. was to receive the Charter of King *John*, and the King's Court or Bench in *Ireland* was to receive the Statute of *Merton*, I will agree that *Parliaments* in *Ireland* may have received Laws in the time of *E.* 2. but there's no colour to believe that they then pretended to more, in relation to *Acts of Parliament*, ſent over to them at large under the Great Seal of *England*.

The

of the Dependency of Ireland.

The Reign of E. 3. I may divide into Three Periods, 1. Before, 2. At, 3. After the main and most express Charter, for a *Parliament* in *Ireland*, of any yet cited, or appearing.

Of Ireland's *being bound by Parliaments of* England, *in the Reign of* E. 3.

1. In the Statute Roll of the beginning of *E.* 3. there are several entries in Latin of this kind. " Mem. " that those Statutes were sent into " *Ireland* in the (a) *form of a Patent*, " with a certain Writ here following. But the entry of the Writ is sometimes omitted, it being look'd on as matter of common form.

(a) In forma Patenti.

In the 2*d.* of that King, a Statute was made at *Northampton*, giving a command about *Fairs*, to all Sheriffs of *England*, and other Parts. In the 6*th.* a Statute was made, supplying the Defects of that Statute, and creating the Forfeiture of double the Value of what should be sold in any *Fair*, or *Market*, beyond the time limited for them in the Charters.

Vid. Rastals Collect.ed. Anno 1572.

Et per ailours.

L 4 In

In the 6*th.* of that King, this last *(a) Statute,* and *all other Statutes made in his Reign to that time,* are sent, *in the form of a Patent,* to *Anthony de Lucy, Justice* of *Ireland,* requiring that those Statutes, and all the Articles therein contained, be Proclaimed in the King's *Land* of *Ireland,* as well *within Liberties,* as without; and that he should cause so much of them as concern'd the *(b) Justice,* and the *People of that Land,* to be *firmly kept,* and *observed.*

A Statute *(c)* 11. of *E.* 3. provides, That, except the King and his Children, no Person, great nor small, within *England, Ireland,* and *Wales,* or so much of *Scotland* as was then *under the King's power,* should wear any Cloth, but what was made in *England, Ireland, Wales,* or such part of *Scotland*; upon pain of *Forfeiture* of the Cloth, and being *Punish'd at the King's pleasure.*

And whereas Mr. *M.* according to the use which he makes of publications, in or by Parliaments in *Ireland,* of Laws made in *Parliaments of England,* would infer, that no Statutes

(a) Rot. Stat. Mem. quod istud Stat. cum Stat. precedentibus temp. Regis E. 3. Post conquestum missa sunt in Hiber. in formâ Patenti cum brevi seq.
(b) Et quantum ad vos & populum nostrum illar. ter. attinet firmiter teneri & observari fac.
(c) Stat. 11. E. 3. c. 2.

tutes made here against *Provisors*, could be of force in *Ireland* till the 32d. of *H.* 6. when 'twas Enacted there, That all those Laws made in *England*, as well as in *Ireland*, be had and kept in force; 'tis evident, that (a) *E. 3d*'s *Parliament* and his *Council* acting in *Parliament*, held, that there was no need of other publishing and enforcing those Laws, than was usual by virtue of the Great Seal of *England*.

P. 68.

(a) Rot. Parl. 20. E. 3. Ut memini, parte transcripti circa idem tempus amissa.

The *Commons* (b) Petitioned, that the *Provisions* and *Ordinances* made in the Parl. 17. of that King, concerning *Provisions* and *Reservations* from the *See of Rome*, be *affirmed by a Statute to endure for ever*: And particularly, (c) that if any *Arch-Bishop*, or other Spiritual Patron, do not present within Four Months after Voidance, by a Man's accepting any Benefice from the *See of Rome*, the *Right of Patronage should accrue to the King*: And they pray, (d) that *Commissions* and *Writs* be sent to all *ports* of *England*, *Wales*, and *Ireland*, and other Places within every County, as there should be occasion, to Apprehend

(b) N. 33.

(c) N. 34.

Note, *This was a disposing of Property.*

(d) N. 37.

hend all those who should carry any of the *Bulls, Process,* or *Instruments* then complained of.

(e) Resp. N. 39.

The Answer in *French* is thus, (e) " 'Tis *accorded* and *assented* by the " *King,* the *Earls, Barons, Justices,* " and other *Sages of the Law,* that " the Things above-written be done, " and in reasonable form, *according* " *to the prayer of the Commons.*

Upon which, there's no doubt but either a *Writ* was sent to *Ireland,* with this Act of Parliament, in the form of a *Charter,* to warrant Commissions for that purpose in *Ireland;* or otherwise, Commissions might issue from hence, to apprehend such Offenders as should be found there.

Stat. Stap. 27. E. 3. c. 1. & 3.

The Statute of the Staple, 27. *E.* 3. taking notice of the Damages to the People of the *King's Realm,* and of *his* Lands of *Wales* and *Ireland,* because the *Staples* had been held out of the *said Realm,* and *Lands,* appoints places for the *Staple* in *Ireland,* as well as in *England* and *Wales;* and creates a *Forfeiture* of the Wool, and other Staple Commodities, which any *English, Irish,* or *Welsh,* should carry

carry out of the said *Realm*, and *Lands*: with the like Penalty, if they should receive Gold or Silver for them, elsewhere than at the respective *Staples*.

<small>Note, *The Wisdom of that Law.*</small>

At which Staples 'tis to be observed, that there were paid Duties and Customs, granted by *Parliament* in England.

Another *Statute*, of the same Year, appoints, That all *Wines* in *England*, *Ireland*, and *Wales*, be Gauged, on pain of *Forfeiture*, and further Punishment at *the King's pleasure*.

<small>27. E. 3. c. 7.</small>

And but Two Years before, the *Statute of Treasons*, which does not name *Ireland*, was made for a Law to the whole Realm, and for *Ireland* as part of it: But none of the King's Subjects in *Ireland* were within that Law, unless they were to be adjudged Subjects of the *Realm of England*. And yet this *Statute* is ordered to be *published* and *observed* in *Ireland*, as well as *England*, in this manner.

<small>Stat. 25, E. 3.

Rot. Stat. M. 15.
For the Honour of God and of Holy Church, and the Amendment of his Realm.</small>

(*a*) "To the Sheriff of *Kent*, "greeting. We send you, *under our* "*Seal*, certain *Statutes*, *made in our* "*Parliament assembled at Westminster*, "on

<small>(*a*) Rot. Stat. de temp. E. 1. E. 2. E. 3. M. 15. De Proclamatione Statuti.</small>

"on the Feast of St. *Hillary* last past,
"by *us*, the *Prelates, Dukes, Earls,*
"*Barons*, and others of the *Common-*
"*alty of our Realm of* England, to the
"said Parliament summoned: Com-
"manding, that you cause the said
"*Statutes* to be read in your *full*
"*County*; and that they be *firmly*
"*observed, and kept.* *Teste* the King
"at *Westm.* the 6th. day of *May.*

(*b*) Consimiles literæ diriguntur Justic. Hib. mutatis mutandis sub eâdem datâ. *P.* 161.

(*b*) "The *like Writs*, of the same
"Date, are sent to the *Justice of Ireland*, what ought to be changed
"being changed.

But if the *Parliaments* of *England* had, or exercised any Jurisdiction or Authority over *Ireland* hitherto; at least, 'tis to be thought, that 'twas all taken from 'em by a Charter of *E*. 3. part of which he transcribes out of Mr. *Prynn*, but for his satisfaction, I shall give him more of it from the

Rot. Pat. 17. R. 2. p. 1. m. 34.

Record, now to be seen in the *Tower*, 'tis a Charter of *R*. 2. of an *Ordinance* for the State of *Ireland*, reciting and confirming the Charter 31. *E*. 3. beginning thus:

Quia

of the Dependency of Ireland.

Quia ex frequenti fide dignor insinuatione accepimus, quod terra nra Hiberniæ,ecclesiaq;Hibernica, ac clerus & populus ejusdem nobis subditus; ob defectum boni regiminis, ac per negligentiam & in curiam Ministror regior ibin,*tam major*,quam minor,hactenus turbati fuerint multipliciter & gravati : Marchiæq; terræ ipsius juxta hostes positæ, per hostiles invasiones vastatæ, occisis Marchionibus, & deprædatis, & eorum habitationibus enormiter *concrematis*, cæterisq; coactis loca propria deserere,quibusdam videlicet ad hostes, cæteris ad loca extranea fugientibus. Diversæq; partes dictar.Marchiar. taliter desolatæ & de-

Because from the frequent Relations of Persons to be credited, we understand that our Land of Ireland, and the Irish Church, and the Clergy, and People subject to us, thro' defect of good Government, and by the negligence and carelesness of the King's Officers there, both great and small, has hitherto been manifoldly troubled and aggriev'd, and the Marches of that land plac'd against the Enemies wasted, the Marches being kill'd and despoil'd,& their Houses enormously burnt, and the rest being forc'd to forsake their habitations,some flying to the Enemies, and others to Foreign Parts. And divers parts of the said Marches so desolated and forsaken, have been possess'd by those Enemies,

The suppos'd Magna Charta for Parliaments in Ireland.

Rot. Stat. ordinatione pro Statu. Hibn.

relictæ, per hostes eosdem occupatæ: nostroq; & ejusdem terræ negotia incongruè & inutiliter, leges & approbatæ consuetudines minus debite observatæ, populo nro bonis & rebus suis contra justitiam, legem, & formam Statutor inde editor. diversimode spoliat. paxq; nostra læsa & *minime* custodita. Ac proditores, Latrones, & Malefactores, non sicut convenit castigati: Quorum malorum aliorumq; occasione, majora damna irreparabillia, evenire, quod absit, timentur, nisi præmissis opportunis *remediis occurrat.* Nos desiderantes utili regimini & quieti eorund. terræ & populi providere quæ *sequuntur: proptereà, de assensu consili nostri,* or-

mies, and the Affairs of us and that Land, are incongruously and unprofitably, and the Laws and approved Customs not duly observed; our People being in divers manners spoil'd of their Goods and things, contrary to Justice, Law, *and the form of* Statutes *in those cases provided: And our Peace is broken, and not in the least kept. And Traytors, Robbers, & Malefactors not punish'd as they ought: By occasion of which, and other Evils, greater irreparable Damages, which, God forbid, are feared as likely to happen, unless the Premises meet with opportune Remedies: We desiring to provide for the convenient Government & Quiet of that* Land, *& People; therefore we by the* consent of our

of the Dependency of Ireland.

dimanda duximus, & firmiter observanda. In prim. viz. volumus & præcipimus, quod sancta Hibernica ecclesia, suas libertates, liber. & consuetudines illæsas habeat, & eis liberè gaudeat & utatur. Item volumus & præcipimus quod nostra, & ipsius terræ negotia & ardua, in consiliis, per peritos consiliarios nostros, ac prælatos & magnates & quosdam de discretioribus, & probatioribus hominibus de *Partibus Vicinis*, ubi ipsa consilia teneri contigerit, *propter hoc evocandos.* In Parliamentis vero per ipsos Consiliarios nros, ac Prelatos & Proceres aliosq; de terra nostra prout mos, exigit, secundum justitiam, legem, consuetudinē, & rationem, tra-

our Council, *have thought fit to provide these following Particulars to be* ordain'd, *and* observ'd : *In the first place, that the Holy* Irish *Church have its Liberties, & free Customs unhurt, and enjoy & use them freely. Also, we will and command, That the Affairs and Arduous Matters of us and that Land, in Councils by our Learned Counsellors, and Prelates, and great Men, and some of the more Discreet & Honest of the parts neighbouring upon the place, where those Counsels shall happen to be held,* to be summoned for this purpose ; *But in the Parliaments by those our Counsellours and Prelates, Peers, and others of our Land, as custom requires, be according to Justice*

ctentur, deducantur,   *ſtice, Law, Cuſtom,*
& fideliter, timore   *and Reaſon, brought,*
favore odio aut pre-   *and faithfully, Fear,*
tio poſtpoſitis, diſcu-   *Favour, Hatred or*
tiantur, & etiam   *Price, being diſre-*
terminentur.   *garded, diſcuſſed, and*
                              alſo determined.

Then particular Proviſions are made here, notwithſtanding the Allowance of *Parliaments* there: Among which,

(*a*) per Juſticiar & Concilium noſtrum Hiberniæ.
    1. That Men guilty of Broakage, ſhould be Puniſhed by the *Juſtice* and *Council* of *Ireland*, and *fined*, and *amoved* from their Offices ; as ſhould ſeem reaſonable to the *Juſtice* and *Counſel.*

(*b*) Statut. & artic. per nos in Parliamentis & aliis magnis conſiliis ad utilitatem populi nri editor. & factor.
    2. That no *Purveyance* be taken contrary to the form of (*b*) *Statutes* and *Articles, made* and *publiſhed*, for the profit of his People, in *Parliaments,* and other *great Councils.* But if there be any force in Mr. *M*'s way of Arguing, the Statutes againſt *Purveyors* were not binding to *Ireland* till 18. *H*. 6. when 'tis Enacted, " *By* " *a Statute made in* Ireland, *that all* " *the Statutes made in* England *againſt* " *the* Extortions and Oppreſſions of " *Pur-*

Purveyers are to be holden and kept in all points, and put in Execution in this *Land of Ireland*.

3. It provides against Robberies, and for Hue-and-Crys, according to the *Statute* of *Winchester*.

4. That no Pardon be pass'd but in *Parliaments* or *Councils*, by the *assent* and *counsel* of the said *Parliaments*, and *Counsellors*. And that there be no general Pardon: but that the Offences be specified and expressed * *according to the tenor of a certain Statute*, by the King and his Council of *England*, publish'd, and sent to *Ireland* to be observed.

* Juxta tenorem cujusdam Statuti per nos & consilium nostrum Angliæ edit. & missi ad Hiberniam observand.

5. The Charter, taking Notice that *false intelligence* us'd to be sent from *Ireland* to *England*, forbids it under (*b*) *grievous Forfeiture*, declaring, that if, for the future, the *Prelates*, the *great Men, Commonalty*, or *any other*, should misinform the *King and his Council*, they should be duly Punished.

(*b*) Sub gravi foris facturâ Prelati, magnates communitates aut quivis alii.

6. Whereas they us'd to Exhibit against one another, several scandalous and vexatious Libels and Bills, it provides, that they being reduced

to Writing, (c) be, under the Seal of the *Chancellor* for the time being, *transmitted* to the King's *Justice, Chancellor,* and *Treasurer* of *Ireland,* who are thereby impowered to do Justice: but this is by virtue *of the great Seal of* England.

(c) Sub sigillo Cancellar. pro-tempore exi-stentis ad Ju-stic. Cancel. & Thes. nostris Hibern. transmittantur.

7. It Impowers the (d) *Justice,* calling to him the *Chancellor* and *Treasurer,* with some *Prelates* and *Earls,* whom he shall know to be fit, or that they ought to be summoned, to determine the Differences between the *English* of *Irish* Extractions, and which were or should afterwards be of *English.*

(d) Vocatis ad se Cancel. & Thes. nris Hiberniæ cum quibusdam Prel. & Comitibus quos evocandos noverit.

8. It requires the *Justice* and his *Associates,* when there was any (e) *special Cause,* to certifie to the *King & his Council of England,* the Names of all Persons guilty, and their Offences.

(e) Ex certa causa sub sigil. Justic. & sibi associator.

Since Mr. *M.* having, as he fancied, (a) *clearly made it out,* that (b) for *Ireland* to be *bound by Acts of Parliament of England,* is against *several Charters of Liberties granted unto the Kingdom of Ireland,* thinks he had no need to *add* any other Authority than

(a) P. 161.
(b) P. 150.

P. 161.

than a piece of that Charter, of the substance of which I have given an Account, with all the distinguishing Expressions; I might well enough close here, and leave it to himself to consider, whether when a *Parliament* is granted, or allowed, to the Land of *Ireland*, in the fullest terms that ever it was in any *King's* Reign, that can be shewn; there was not at the same time a full exercice of the Power of the *Crown* and *Kingdom* of England, in making Laws, and requiring the Execution of others made in *England*, without any desire or expectation of a Ratification there?

And whether even their *Parliaments are not threatned, if they send false intelligence to* England?

For full proof that in this *Ordinance,* the Authority of the *Parliament* of *England* was retein'd and asserted, I must observe to Mr. *M.* that this Noble *Charter* to *Ireland*, is but according to the usual Methods of Publishing Acts of Parliament, put under the great Seal, and thereby made a *Patent* or *Charter*: but 'twas an *Ordinance*

The History and Reasons

-dinance, (a) or *Act*, of *Parliament*, for the *State* of *Ireland*, as may be seen by the Statute Roll.

(a) Vid. Rot. Stat. temp. E. 1. E. 2. E. 3. m. 12.

3. After this Statute mentioning *Parliaments* in *Ireland*, the *Parliament* here exercised the same Authority in making *Ordinances* and *Laws* for *Ireland*, and the *King and his Council* held *Ireland* to be bound by those Laws, as part of the *Realm of England*.

Rot. Stat. sup. m. 8.
Stat. 36. E. 1.

A Statute made in the 36th of that King provides, that no Lord of *England*, nor *any other Person of the Realm*, except the *King* and *Queen*, take *purveyance* on pain of *Life* and *Member*; and takes from Mayors and Constables of *Staples*, all Jurisdiction in Criminal Causes: but I do not find any mention of *Ireland*, and yet that both King and Council judged, that the publishing them in *Ireland* would avail as much as the publishing them in *England*, appears by the Writ to the Sheriff of *Essex* and *Hertfordshire*, requiring him to publish the *Statutes* and *Ordinances* then made by the King, with the *common assent* of the *Prelates*,

M. 7. De Statuto proclamando.

of the Dependency *of* Ireland.

Prelates, great Men, and *Commonalty,* in his *(a) full Parliament* at *Westminster* ; and to return the Writ, with an Account of the Execution of it to the King in his *Chancery.*

(b) This Writ is tested by the King.

And in *(c)* the same manner commands are sent to the *Justice of Ireland.*

But notwithstanding this Transmission to *Ireland* of Statutes made here, one of which is about *Purveyance,* which is at least the Second of this kind made to bind *Ireland,* Mr. *M.* may if he pleases, hold, that this was not Law in *Ireland,* till *(d)* 18. *H.* 6.

But after all, I would intreat the favour of Mr. *M.* to inform me, whether, according to himself, such Acts of Parliament in *Ireland,* were needful to Confirm Laws made here; when, if he puts a right construction upon the Record above cited, * 9 *E.* 1. and of the Record, † 50 *E.* 3. of a Writ from hence for the Expences of *the Men of* Ireland,

(a) In pleno Parl. nro apud Westm.

(b) Per ipsum Regem & Consilium.

(c) Eodem modo mandatum est singulis vicecom. per Angl. Ep. Dunelm Edw. Pr. Walliæ & Com. Cestriæ Rob. de Harle Constab. Castri Dover & Custod. 5 port. & Justic. Hiberniæ.

(d) P. 68. *Of the fancy that the* Irish *had Representatives chosen in* Ireland, *and sent from thence to be Members of Parliament here.*

* P. 95.
† P. 97.

who

who last came over to serve in Parliament in England; The Men of *Ireland* us'd to send their Representatives hither, to the making the Laws by which they were to be bound: till ‖ "this sending of Representatives out of *Ireland* to the Parliaments of *England*, was found in process of time to be very troublesome and inconvenient."

‖ P. 98.

But whatever Mr. *M.* may imagin in this matter, that sort of representation of *Ireland* in the Parliaments of *England*, was no more than they had in the time of *H.* 3. and have 'tis likely generally had to this day, of persons entrusted to sollicit the Affairs of *Ireland*, upon their numerous Petitions to the King, and his Council in Parliament; for which Receivers and Triers used to be appointed, or other matters of concern to them. But whether they were chosen by their * Parliaments, when they had them, or elsewhere, their Expences, as appears by the Record cited by Mr. *M.* were levied by Authority under the Great Seal of *England.*

Vid. Rot. Parl. de temp. E. 3.

* Vid. Rot. Pat. 5. R. 2. part 2. m. 19. *Their Parliament required to send Nuncios.*
P. 97.

But

of the Dependency of Ireland.

But I will shew a Record of the time of *H.* 3. when I will agree, that they had (*a*) *Nuntii, Messengers*, deputed, as 'tis likely, from a Parliament in *Ireland*.

H. 3. in his Writ, or Letter, to the Barons of *Ireland,* takes notice, that, by the (*b*) *advice of his People*, he had given a favourable answer to some of their requests, made known by persons deputed from them. But because those persons alledged, that their Instructions were to insist upon all the particulars of their Requests; the King sends a Precept to the *Justice* of *Ireland,* under the *Great Seal* of *England,* requiring him, as it seems, to summon a *Parliament*; for, he was carefully to open the matters before the *Barons* of *Ireland,* and to know what they would give for the Liberties they desired.

The *Justice* had no Authority to have those Liberties setled in a *Parliament* there, but was to signify their Answer to the *King*; upon which the *King* would do what should be fitting, without taking any Right from them.

(*a*) Rot. claus. 32 H.3. m.6.d. Rex Baronibus Hiberniæ.

(*b*) De nostrorum consilio.
(*c*) Nuntii ex parte vestrâ.

Ut eisdem articulis vobis diligenter expositis, &c.

Et nos præd. negotium ad nostrum & vestrum honorem effectui mancipare curabimus sine ex heredatione vestrâ.

That

The History and Reasons

That this was to be done in *Parliament* here, and that the *Messengers* from *Ireland* were no Members of that *Council* of the *King's People* which sent the Answer, is beyond dispute; nor is there colour to believe, that any of their *Deputies*, or *Representatives*, had in any King's Reign more to do here, than those of the time of *H.* 3. had.

P. 96.

But surely no Man but Mr. *M.* will conclude, that such Instances, or the mention of the *Consent*, or *Petition* of the Irish in some Particulars, manifestly shew, that *the King and Parliament of* England, *would not enact Laws to bind* Ireland, *without the concurrence of the Representatives of that Kingdom.*

P. 85, 98.

Since therefore I have proved to the contrary, from *H.* 2's first acquisition, till towards the latter end of *E.* 3. and Mr. *M.* declares, that he will *consider the more antient Precedents of English Statutes which particularly name* Ireland, *and are therefore said to be of force* in that Kingdom; I might rest here, did not Mr. *M.*

of the Dependency of Ireland.

M. take notice of the Statute of the Staple, 2 *H*. 6. and the Resolution of the Judges upon it, 1 *H*. 7. in such a manner as makes it requisite to be set in a truer Light.

Of the Statute of the Staple, 2 H. 6. *and the Resolution of the Judges upon it.*

The Merchants of *Waterford*, pursuant to the Licence granted them by E. 3. and confirmed by *E.* 4. had carried Wool, contrary to the ordinary provision of the Statute 2 *H.* 6. which being seized by the Treasurer of *Calais* as forfeited, part to the King, and part to himself as discoverer; The Merchants by Bill in the *Exchequer* here, pray restitution. 'Tis to be observed, that the Act upon which the Wool was seized, tho it creates a forfeiture of the value of Wool, Butter, Cheese, and other staple Commodities, carried from *England*, *Ireland*, and *Wales*, to other parts than *Calais*, and gives the Informer a 4*th* of what shall be carried contrary to that Act, from any County of the *Realm*, makes no mention of *Ireland* as to the Informers share; and therefore his Interest

Pais du Roialm.

rest could bear no debate, unless *Ireland* had been included, and the *Counties* of *Ireland* were *Counties*, within the Realm of *England*.

P. 90. But Mr. *M.* says, the 2d Question was, *Whether the King could grant his Licence contrary to the Statute, and especially where the Statute gives half the Forfeiture to the Discoverer.* But

Salve la Prerogative le Roy.

he might have observed, that the Statute has an express *saving of the King's Prerogative*, which goes thrô the whole, and certainly related to the *King*'s granting Licences to the contrary in some particular Cases: Notwithstanding which, 'twas the opinion of the Parliament the next year, that this saving was not sufficient: and therefore the King, at the

3 H. 6. c. 4.

grievous complaint of the Commons, impowers the Chancellor of *England* to give Licences for *Butter* and *Cheese*, at his discretion.

As to the question, Whether *Ireland* was bound by the Stat. 2 *H. 6.* Mr. *M.* pretends to transcribe *verbatim*, what relates to it in the *Year-Book*, 2 *R.3.* The matter, as he observes, was brought

P. 90.

of the Dependency of Ireland.

brought *before all the Judges of England* in the *Exchequer Chamber*; but after [*ibi*] he omits the word [*dicebatur*] it was said, not *per curiam*, but at the most only by some Judg or Judges; and might have been only by one of the Counsel for the Merchants. Whoever then held that *Ireland* was not bound by that Act, might have spoken it in relation to the Informer, who could claim no share of any Forfeiture incur'd from *Ireland*, unles the Counties of *Ireland*, were taken to be Counties within the Realm of *England*: But even as to this matter they were soon convinced of their mistake, in thinking *Ireland* was not bound by that Statute.

Mr. *M.* might have learn'd from the *Year-Book*, 1 *H.* 7. that this was so far from the resolution of the Court 2 *R.* 3. that there was no Judgment, but the Bill fell upon the *demise* of that King; which till the Statute 1 *E.* 6. was a discontinuance of all real, personal, and mix'd Actions commenced in *any of his Majesty's*

P. 91.

1 H. 7.
Note. Ireland *not named, yet the Courts in* Ireland *certainly included.*

sty's Courts, and *other Courts of Record*. And therefore 1 *H.* 7. the Suit was begun again, as if commenced in that King's Reign; and then the queſtion coming before all the Judges in the *Exchequer Chamber*, *Huſſey* the Chief-Juſtice, delivering the Judgment of the Court, declared, with the aſſent of the reſt of the Judges, that *Ireland* was bound by that *Act*, and I leave to Mr. *M.* to make it out, that this was *directly contrary to the Judges* opinion in the 2d of *R.* 3. or that they were *all poſitive, that within the Land of* Ireland, *the Authority of the Parliament of* England *will not affect them*.

If there had been any ſuch opinion, 'twas not delivered as the Judgment of the Court; and however, the Reſolution 1 *H.* 7. has ſetled the Point another way.

This Caſe is abridg'd, and the Reſolution receiv'd for Law by *Brook*, a Learned Judg in the Reign of *H.* 8. without any *query*, which is uſual where he doubted: his *tamen nota*, that *Ireland is a Kingdom by it ſelf*, and has

1 H. 7. f. 3.

Come bill. fait en temps le Roy que ore eſt.

P. 92, 93.

Vid. Brook. tit. Parl. ſec. 90.

of the Dependency of Ireland.

has Parliaments of its own, implies no more than that this, tho objected 2 *R*. 3. was of no weight to alter that judgment; and is as much as to say, a Kingdom may be distinct from the Crown of a Kingdom to which it is annexed, and have Parliaments at home; and yet be govern'd by the *Statute Laws* of that other Kingdom as subordinate to it. And tho the naming that subordinate Kingdom in an Act of Parliament here, or the otherwise manifesting an intention to bind it, is *no step towards obtaining* a Parliamentary consent in *Ireland*; yet 'tis towards the submission and acquiescence of the People to those Laws, by which they and their Forefathers had consented to be governed.

P.118. *Is Ireland's being named in an English Act of Parliament, the least step towards the obtaining the consent of the people of* Ireland?

I may now leave it to Mr. *M*. to answer his own Questions, *Shall* Ireland *receive Charters of Liberties, and be no partakers of the freedoms therein contained? or do these words signify in* England *one thing, and in* Ireland *no such thing?*

P. 157.

Nor need I much fear his terrible Expostulation, *Whether it be not against natural Equity and Reason, that a Kingdom regulated within it self,*

P. 155.

and

and having its own Parliaments, should be bound, without their consent, by the Parliament of another Kingdom? But I should hope that he will admit it to be against *natural Reason*, to go away with a Conclusion, without some colour of proving the Premises; and therefore before he had laid it home (*a*) to English hearts to consi-

(*a*) P. 105.

der, *Whether Proceedings only of thirty seven years standing, shall be urged against a Nation, to deprive them of the Rights and Liberties which they enjoyed for five hundred years before*; He would have done well to have proved, that any one *Century*, or much less number of years, for these five hundred years & more, *Ireland* was ever, according to the terms of his own Question, *regulated within it self*; or, that 'tis a *Kingdom* of more than (*b*) one hundred and sixty years standing.

(*b*)From 33 H. 8. An. 1542. at soonest.

* P. 105.

But it seems just * *thirty seven years since*, and never before, the *Rights* and *Liberties* which they had quietly *enjoyed* till then, were *invaded*, and from that day to this have been constantly complained of. 'Tis not to be ex-

expected, that a man who remembers so little of those many Acts of Parliament made in *Ireland*, which might have moderated his assurance in this matter, should keep in memory even his own concessions to the contrary; as where he grants, that the Parliaments of *England* did at least claim a superiority, before the 10*th* of *H.* 4. and 29 *H.* 6.

P. 65, 66.

P. 68.

But then he says, *We have not one single Instance of an English Act of Parliament, expresly claiming this right of binding us; but we have several Instances of Irish Acts of Parliament expresly denying this Subordination.*

Object.

Answ. 1. As to the express claiming an Authority to do what is done, by virtue of an Authority always suppos'd; that's so far from an *Argument* against it, that it shews 'twas never call'd in question.

2. No *Act* of *Parliament*, even in *Ireland*, can be shewn or pretended, denying the *Subordination*; not but that there might be some question of the general binding, for want of due pub-

publication, either under the Great Seal of *England*; or of otherwise knowing the Intention of the Parliament of *England*: This, not the Authority, was the *Ambiguity* mentioned in the Statute of *Ireland*, 8 *E*. 4. in relation to a Statute 6 *R*. 2. which, without naming *Ireland*, alters a Law that did name it.

P. 79.

3. If there were such *Act* of *Parliament* in *Ireland*, 13 *E*. 2. as 'tis supposed that a certain Judg in *Ireland* had seen, and that we might rely upon his Judgment in the sense of it; receiving some Laws before that time made in *England*, and suspending the execution of others; what I have shewn above from undoubted Records, may be enough to shew, that this would not in the least weaken the Right of the Parliament of *England*, exercised before and after that time: And if there were another Statute, 10 *H*. 4. that no Laws should be of force, unless they were allow'd and publishsed by a Parliament in *Ireland*: This, tho 'tis a strain farther than 'tis likely any Parliament of *Ireland* ever yet went, would

P. 63, 64.

of the Dependency of Ireland.

would not necessarily infer any more, than that the Laws made in *England* should be thus published, to the end they might be more generally known; not but that the intention of the Parliament of *England*, made known under the great Seal of *England*, was as much to be obeyed as their own Record shews that 'twas 29. *E.* 1.   Vid. sup. Davis f. 21. b.

The Authorities above-cited having manifested the several Titles which the *Crown* and *Kingdom* of *England* have to the Land of *Ireland*; and that from the 18*th.* of *H.* 2. at the latest, downwards as far as Mr. *M.* makes any controversie, neither the *Irish Nation,* nor the *English* there, have been govern'd without the interposition of the *Parliament of England;* and that the *Parliament* of *Ireland* had all its Laws made here, or derived under Authority from hence, and that not from the *King's alone,* or the *Kings* and *their Privy Counsels,* but their Parliament; that the *Parliaments* of *Ireland* have had no Provision for their being holden   An. 1172.

N

den within any certain time, nor ever had Authority given them to act as *independent on the Parliament of England*; I may well conclude, that the right of the *Parliament* of *England* to bind *Ireland* by Laws made here, without any *Members* chosen for *Ireland*, is so far from being departed from, that 'tis *strengthened* and *confirmed* by the *continual usage* of the *Parliaments* of *England*, and *submission* of the *Parliaments and People of Ireland*: to which 'twill be needless to add the consideration of the *inestimable Treasure* spent in several Ages, for maintaining the *English Interest* there; and the late freeing it from an *Universal Insurrection*, and *Usurpation*.

His Politicks and seeming popular notions wrong, and misapplyed.

4. Having us'd the proper means to convince Mr. *M.* by the true *argumentum ad hominem*, shewing that the chief Weapons which he uses turn strongly against himself; I need the less apprehend the natural force of his reasoning upon dry Notions.

The

The right says he, which *England* may pretend to *for binding us by their Acts of Parliament, can be founded only on the imaginary Title of Conquest, or Purchase, or on Precedents and Matters of Record.* p. 4.

Wherein he admits, that *Precedents and Matters of Record*, may give a *Right*, which is neither by *Conquest* nor *Purchase*: and of this the Authors he refers to might satisfie him at large. I'll agree with him, that *on consent depends the obligation of all humane Laws: insomuch that without it, by the unanimous Opinions of all Jurists no sanctions are of any force.* p. 150, 151.

But do any of them say that the *consent* is necessary to be *exprest*, and that *immediate?* if it were the Sons could not be bound by those Laws which their Fathers chose, in restriction of *natural liberty*; and he might have observ'd, by his own Authors, and even in the Words cited by himself, that *approbation, not only Men give, who personally declare their assent, by Voice, Sign, or act; but also when others do it in their* p. 152. Hooker l. 1. sec. 10.

their names, by right originally at least derived from them, as in Parliaments, Councils, &c.

He adds, *To be commanded we do consent, when that Society whereof we are part, hath at any time before consented.* Farther yet, whatever *Freedoms* the Progeny of the *English* and *Britains* now in *Ireland* claim with the *natural Born Subjects* of England, *as being descended from them;* 'tis certain, every Man here does not, as an *English-man*, claim to be a *Member of Parliament*, or to have a Voice in chusing one: But there are many without this Privilege, who have been concluded by the *consent of their Forefathers,* and their own; agreeing to stay within a Kingdom govern'd by such Laws, to which they owe *Obedience* and *Submission*, at least as long as they will receive the benefit of them, and the *protection* which they assure.

This is the case of those *Englishmen*, who chuse to live in *Ireland*, under the *Protection of England*; without which the Protestants there

of the Dependency of Ireland.

there could not have subsisted, in any Age since the *Reformation*: and if the *Irish Natives* are not *conquer'd*, or the Right of *Conquest* over them, ought not to be carryed beyond the reparation of the *Damages* sustained from them; or if *a just conquest gets no power, but only over those who have actually assisted in that unjust force*; and if the right of conquest *extends little farther, than over the Lives of the Conquer'd, but their posterity can lose no benefit thereby*: If an outragious and Brutal Enemy, may not be restrain'd from doing farther mischief, by the taking from him that Power and Estate which would enable him to carry on his Designs; if the posterity may not suffer in the consequence of this, as the aggressor's property is become the *Conquerer's*; if the Children may not be restrain'd from revenging their Father's Quarrel; let the *English* in *Ireland* look to it, how to justifie those Possessions which they enjoy, by the help of the Crown and Kingdom of *England,*

P. 24.
P. 20.
P. 21.

land: and if their Consciences are squeamish, let them renounce their Right to the Lands of the Natives; but let them not bring in to question the Right of *Engl.* to all Foreign Plantations: and let them never fear that equal Power here, to which a great part of the *English Nation* are resigned, without any other kind of *consent*, than the People of *Ireland* have given, to the Laws made in *England*, with intention to bind them, and be published there.

As to his notion of *Purchase*; whenever *Ireland* will repay the value of the Purchase, that *inestimable* and *infinite* expence of *Men*, *Money*, *Victuals*, and *Arms*, which their own Parliaments own to have protected and supported them for several Ages; there's no great question but *England* would be willing to leave 'em to their own ways.

Whereas he will suppose, that the Authority, which the *Lords* and *Commons* of *England* have exercised from Age to Age, in relation

Vid. P. 143.
The People of England ought to be fully repy'd.

Prerog.

tion to *Ireland*, would imply that the Parliament of *England* have claim'd *a coordinate Power with the King*; what is this but to argue, that in relation to *England* the *Parliament* is *coordinate*? however, as by Parliament he means only the *States* of the Kingdom; 'tis evident this infinuation proceeds from his not obferving the *Gothick conftitution*, for which he would be thought very zealous: but might have known, that the *States of the Kingdom*, or the *ordines regni*, are thofe who are entituled to meet the King in Perfon, or by *reprefentation*, in *his Parliaments*; where *the King is a diftinct Body Politick* by himfelf: and, having the Supremacy, is manifeftly above the *ordines regni*. P. 166.

But tho' the Head which Mr. *M*. raifes, about the fuppos'd injury to *Prerogative*, be only upon a pretended *coordinate* Power with the King, he carries it farther: and will have it, that for the *States of this Realm* to ufe an Authority, tho' *fubordinate* to the King, to introduce P. 166, 167.

duce new *Laws*, or repeal old, establish'd in *Ireland*, is a violation of the *Constitution of Ireland* under *Boyning's Act*, and of the *Prerogative of the Crown of England*; which he supposes to have been highly advanced by that Statute speaking of the effect of which he says,

"The King's Prerogative is ad-
"vanced to a much higher pitch
"than ever was challeng'd by the
"*King's in England*, and the *Par-*
"*liament* of *Ireland* stands almost
"*on the same bottom as the King*
"*does in* England: *I say, almost*
"*on the same bottom*; for the *Irish*
"*Parliament* have not only a Ne-
"gative (as the King has in *Eng-*
"*land*) to whatever Laws the *King*
"and his *Privy Councils* of both,
"or either *Kingdom*, shall lay be-
"fore them; but have also a li-
"berty of proposing to the *King*
"and his *Privy Council* here, such
"Laws as the *Parliament* of *Ire-*
"*land* think expedient to be pass'd:
"which Laws being thus propo-
"sed to the *King*, and put into
"form, and transmitted to the *Par-*
liament

of the Dependency of Ireland.

"*liament* here of *Ireland,* accor-
"ding to *Poyning's Act* must be
"pass'd or rejected in the very
"words, even to a little, as they
"are laid before our *Parliament*;
"we cannot alter the least *Iota*.

In this Narrative of their *Constitution* under that Law, he has omitted the mentioning what is very material, that the *Kings* answer to what they propose, is to be transmitted *under the great Seal of England*, and this is to be the *Licence and Authority* for the holding a *Parliament* in *Ireland*; and therefore their Acts of *Parliament* since that settlement, mention their being held *by Authority under the Great Seal of* England. 3. C. 4. P. M. Vid. etiam *Mr. M.* p. 160. of *the Stat.* 10. H. 7.

And there were two obvious ends and effects of this Law, as Mr. *M.* himself owns, 1. "*The pre-*
"*vention of any thing passing in the*
"*Parliament of* Ireland *surrepti-*
tiously, to the prejudice of the King or the English Interest of Ireland: to which I must add, *or of* England. P. 160.

2. To

2. To take from the *Irish* there, all colour of pretence of holding *Parliaments* as an *independent Kingdom* by virtue of any Authority *within that Land.*

But how the King's *Prerogative in the Legiſlature* was advanced by this I do not underſtand: ſince long before, as well as notwithſtanding this ſuppoſed *Conſtitution* of an *Independent Parliament*, held by *Authority from the Great Seal of* England; the King had, and has, the *Prerogative*, not only to diſſolve the *Iriſh Parliaments* at his Pleaſure; but never to call any: which this *Gentleman* ought to fear, leaſt ſuch a claim as he makes might occaſion: and I would gladly know, what part of *their Conſtitution* provides for the *frequent holding of Parliaments in* Ireland: yet frequency of Parliaments in *England*, is an undoubted part of the *Fundamental Conſtitution* of the *Engliſh Monarchy.*

Farther, is it any *advance* to the *Prerogative in the Legiſlature*, that a Prince who has the full exerciſe of an an *absolute Legiſlature at home,* is only poſſeſſed of a Proviſion againſt having any attempt made, to the leſſening that his *ſettled* and *indubitable* Prerogative?

I muſt needs ſay this *Gentleman* has a way of arguing beyond my apprehenſion: for I cannot ſee the conſequence, how the *Prerogative* ſhould be advanced, if, as he will have it, the *Iriſh Parliament is put almoſt on the ſame bottom,* as that the *King ſtands* on in *England*: if it be ſo, I ſhould think it a leſſening of the *Prerogative,* to have an *Iriſh Parliament* almoſt *coordinate* with him: which Mr. *M.* is very fearful leaſt an *Engliſh Parliament* ſhould pretend to.

And I as little underſtand the reaſon he gives, why the *Parliament* of *Ireland ſtands almoſt upon the ſame bottom with the King;* for ſays he, they have not only a *Negative Vote* as the King has in *England,* but liberty to propoſe; yet the Laws muſt be paſs'd or rejected without alteration: This I take to be Foreign to the *bottom on which*

which, either the *King* or that *Parliament, stands.* If it be meant that they are, in a manner, as absolute in this *negative* and *liberty of purposing,* as the King is in *England:* since it relates only to Laws first desired from *Ireland,* either by the *Privy Council,* or *Parliament* there; this *Constitution* of their *Parliament,* is so far from giving them a negative to the Laws pass'd in *England,* with declared intention to bind them in *Ireland,* that the Authority of *England* is wove into the very Constitution; and the Parliaments of *Ireland* own that Authority by their very Sitting and Enacting.

Mr. *M.* having represented that Constitution of their Parliaments, by which he thinks they *stand almost upon the same bottom as the King* did here, makes this strong assumption.

If therefore the *Legislature* of
" *Ireland* stand on this foot in re-
" lation to the *King* and to the Par-
" *liament* of *Ireland;* and the *Parliament*

"ment of England *do remove it from this bottom, and assume it to themselves,* where the King's Prerogative is much narrower, and as it were reversed (for there *the King* has only a negative Vote) I humbly conceive 'tis an encroachment on the King's Prerogative.*

But he might consider,

1. That as here by the *Parliament* he takes *Lords* and *Commons* without the *King*; he mistakes the Fact in relation to their exercice of Power: for they do not *assume* to themselves the Power of making any Law, but *with,* and *under the King*.

2. Neither do they, in the highest exercice of their Power, take from the *Irish* any thing allowed or directed by *Poyning's Law*, or any other *Constitution*.

3. They do but assert the *Chief Prerogative of the Crown of* England, by which, *due consent being had,* our Kings give Laws to this *Realm,* and all the Dominions belonging to it.

4. The

4. The ancient course of the Proceedings of the Parliaments of *England*, and their making all manner of Provisions for the Government of *Ireland*, evince, that *Poyning*'s Law was rather an Indulgence to the *English* there, directing a Method for their maintaining the face of a *Legiſlature* among themſelves, than any reſtraint of Power before veſted in the Parliaments of England. And after all, this Law was never, as I take it, confirm'd by a Parliament of *England*. I muſt not here omit the conſequences which Mr. *M*. draws, from the *Parliament* of *England*'s pretending Power to impoſe any one Law upon *Ireland*.

P. 170.

1. That 'twill *naturally introduce* the Taxing them without their conſent.

P. 171.

2. That 'twill leave the People of *Ireland* in the *greateſt confuſion* imaginable: that they are not *permitted to know*, which is the *Supreme Authority* which they are bound to obey; whether the Parliament of England, or that of Ireland

of the Dependency of Ireland.

land *or both* ; *and that the uncertainty is or may be made a pretence for disobedience.*

3. That 'twill be *highly inconvenient for* England ; *may make the Lords and* People *of* Ireland *think they are not well used, and may drive them into Discontent.* Pag. 172.

1. Not here to consider, how far the *Lordship* of the *Land* of *Ireland* may infer the Taxing it; if it should refuse to concur as it ought, to its own Preservation : since the Law of necessity is no farther to be used, or considered, than while the necessity is apparent; I may say, that this is no consequence to be apprehended, and that as the Right of Taxing, does not follow from the Right of Governing; and the Nature of the Government depends upon the first *Submission*, and that *Interpretation* and *Confirmation* of it, which both the *governing* Nation, and the *governed* have put upon it: I must infer, with deference to the *National Authority*, that the Power which *England* has from the time of *H.* 2. claimed and exercised over

Of the Consequence in relation to Taxes.

Ireland,

Ireland, does not *naturally introduce the Taxing them without their con-*

Pag. 88, 89.

sent ; yet, *if the Modern Precedents of* English *Acts of Parliament alledg'd against Mr.* M's Notion, are *Innovations,* and only of

Pag. 105.

Thirty seven Years standing, depriving them *of the Rights and Liberties which they enjoyed for five hundred Years before, and which were invaded without their consent* ; such an Invasion would *naturally introduce the Taxing them without their Consent.*

But since *England* uses no Power which it has not generally used for these 500 Years, he should avoid putting it to the necessity, or temptation to go farther.

Of the uncertainty what Authority to obey.

2. As to the supposed uncertainty where the *Supream Authority* resides ; he might have found that pass'd dispute in their *own Statutes* ; and yet their Denyals could be of no weight, till they had absolutely renounced the *Protection* of *England*; and indeed must be thought to have come in *surreptitiously,* without the due care of the *Governours,*

nours there, under the *Crown* of *England*; as well as without the notice of the Nation which has hitherto *protected* and *supported* them.

However, the Obedience which that Nation has from *H.* 2d's *Time*, pay'd to the Laws of *England*, after they had been duly publiſhed by Authority under the *Great Seal* of England, might have ſufficiently taught them where the *real Legiſlature* is veſted, and by them and their Forefathers acknowledged.

And ſince he admits that till a *Regular Legiſlature* was eſtabliſhed in *Ireland by the* Iriſh *voluntary Submiſſion to, and acceptance of the Laws and Government of* England, *we muſt repute them to have ſubmitted themſelves to the Statute Laws* made under *H.* 2. King *John*, and *H.* 3. and *their Predeceſſors*; If a Kingdom can have *no Supreme within it ſelf*, and a Subordinate Parliament is no Parliament, as he would infer; he muſt thank himſelf for the Conſequence, that therefore they have neither a Kingdom, nor

Pag. 58.

Pag. 165.

a Parliament: and then by his own confession, they are as much to be govern'd by the Statutes now made in *England*, as their *Predecessors* were in the Times of King *John*, and *H. 3*.

Of the supposed Inconvenience to England.

3. As to the imagined Inconvenience to *England*, and almost threatned *Defection* from the Crown of the Kingdom, this *Gentleman*'s Undertaking makes it evident, that the Authority ought the rather to be exerted, to help some Men's Understandings, least such a shew of Arguments, and popular Flourishes, should encourage them to act as if they were a *compleat* Kingdom *within themselves*, with a King at the Head of them, during whose *Absence*, or professing a Religion contrary to that which the generality of the People profess, they might assert the Right of a Free *Kingd. subject to no Man's Laws*, but what they had consented to immediately, or permitted to grow into a Custom.

Since this Gentleman thinks he has silenced all the *Patriots of Liberty*

berty and *Property*, by his warm Appeals to them, and wheadling Notions of the *inherent*, and unalienable Rights of Mankind; and, howevre that he, has engag'd the *Crown* of his fide, by adorning it with a *Prerogative* to govern *Ireland* without any relation to the *publick good* of that *Kingdom*, the *rightful* Poffeffion of which, carries *Ireland* as an Appendant to the *Imperial Crown*;

I muft defire him to confider whether in this, as well as other Particulars before obferved, the Charge of Inconfiftency, will not fall upon him more juftly than upon the Lord *Coke*.

A little to qualifie this heat, upon the fuppos'd Injury to *Prerogative*, or common Right, I fhall recommend thefe Heads to his ferious Confideration.

1. Whether he does not yield, that if there were a *Submiffion* and *Confent*, to fuch Laws for Government, as *England* fhould from time to time publifh, to be obeyed in *Ireland*; this would be no injury

to the *Common Rights of Mankind?*

2. Whether his Tragical Exclamations, against those who have acted contrary to what he takes to be the Right of the *English Proprietors* in *Ireland*, are not founded upon the Supposition; that those *Acts of Parliaments* there, which have been made of late Days, with express intention of binding *Ireland*, are *Innovations?*

3. Whether it being evident, that the Laws made here, have for so many Ages been enforced and submitted to, as binding *Ireland*; an *English-man* in *Ireland* has more reason to complain of a Law made here, than a *Wealthy Merchant Free of no Corporation*, or any *Englishman* whose Profit obliges him to a continuance in Foreign Parts?

4. Whether all the *English* Treasure which has been spent, and Lives lost for the Reduction of *Ireland*, were absolutely at the Disposal of the *Princes*, or directed by any of their Parliaments?

5. Whether a Law Book digested

of the Dependency of Ireland.   213

sted in the Time of *H.* 2. as 'tis suppos'd, by Publick Authority, does not shew, that in the Notion of that very Time, when Mr. *M.* supposes that the Right of the *Crown of* England *over* Ireland, was first acquired, there was, or might be *Treason against the Kingdom of* England, as well as against the *King* ? Vid. Glanvil de Seditione Regis vel Regni inter crimina lesæ Majestatis.

6. Whether the submitting to take the *English Laws* from the *King*, implyed the taking them from him alone; unless he made Laws in *England*, without the Consent of the *States* of the Kingdom of *England* ?

7. Whether if the English *modus tenendi Parliamenta*, being, as Mr. *M.* thinks he has proved, transmitted to *Ireland*, by *H.* 2. stiling himself *Conqueror* of *Ireland*; after that, a Parliament of *Ireland*, held in that form, should have Voted themselves *independant upon the Parliament of* England ; would not every Member have been liable to an *Impeachment for Treason against the King and Kingdom of* England ?   8. If

8. If by Municipal Laws, or the Provision of the Common Law of *England*, in Cases not particularly express'd, the Son may justly suffer in the Consequence of his Father's Forfeiture for Treason; may not the same Reason hold for a *dependent Nation*?

9. Whether *Jurists*, universally agreed to be well skill'd in the Law of Nations, and even such as hold the *People* or *Community* to be the common Subject of Power, do not maintain, that as well the Dominion or Power vested in the People, as that which was in the Prince, may be acquired by another *Prince*, or *State*?

10. Whether they do not hold, that such acquisition made in one Age, and continued, lays an obligation upon Posterity to submit to it?

11. Whether they do not generally hold, that *Protection* is a good foundation of Power; and that this confirms the *Submissions* of *Publick Societies* anciently made, to the Nature of that Government which

which they had subjected themselves to, and to the governing Families?

12. Whether the *Protection* which the stronger Kingdom has continued to give to a weaker, is not at least as forceable an Argument for *Obedience*, as that *protection* which any Nation does, or can receive from the *Prince* who is at the Head of it?

13. Whether our *Saviour*'s Observation upon the *Roman penny*, and St. *Paul*'s Epistle to the *Romans*, did not establish a general Rule of Subjection?

14. Whether the *Jews*, and other Nations subject to the *Roman Empire*, had not much more plausible pretences for casting off the *Roman Yoak*, than the *Irish* have for disowning the *English Legislature*?

15. Whether our Victorious and Heroical *Kings*, *E.* 3. and *H.* 5. thought it any diminution to the *Prerogative of the Crown of* England, for their Parliaments to be joyn'd with them, in giving Terms

Vid. Rot. Parl. temp. E. 3. & H. 5.

to those Parts of *France*, which were brought under the *Crown of England*, in Wars carried on at a National Expence?

16. Whether, notwithstanding his Concession, that every King of *England*, is *ipso facto* King of *Ireland*; the contrary does not follow from his Notion of *Prerogative*, of *Irelands* being a compleat Kingdom regulated within *it self*; and the Supposition that Acts of Parliament in *England* cannot bind *Ireland*, till confirmed by Parliament there?

17. Whether therefore according to his way of arguing, the Subjects of *Ireland*, who fought under King *William*, before he was recognized by a *Parliament* in *Ireland*, then served their *Lawful* and *Rightful King*.

18. Whether to dedicate to His present *Majesty*, a Book of such consequences as the direct Answer to these Questions would manifest, argues a due Opinion of His *Majesty*'s Judgment and Penetration?

FINIS.

ERRATA.

Pag. 5. Lin. 8. *for* have *r.* know, *ib. l.* 14. *r.* grievous, *ib.* p. 7. *l.* 9. *for* must *r.* might, *ib. l.* 18. *r.* you represent, p. 11. *l.* 26. *r.* and nature, p. 12. *l.* 23. *r.* first expedition, p. 29. *l.* 25. *for* will *r.* would, p. 41. *l. ult. for* none *r.* no Charter, p. 62. *l.* 18. *r.* and that, p. 63. *l.* 23. *r.* Jurisdiction which, p. 64. *l.* 25. *r.* from, p. 70. *l.* 5. *r.* would, p. 87. *dele* voluntary, p. 95. *l.* 11. *r.* H. 3. p. 104. *l.* 13. *for* the *r.* that, p. 108. *l.* 6. *r.* here, p. 112. *l.* 4. *r.* when, p. 115. *l.* 12. *dele* chief, p. 122. *l.* 20. *r.* carta, p. 133. *l.* 1. *r.* be then, p. 134. *l.* 1. *r.* there then, *ib. l.* 9. *for* me *r.* him, p. 139. *l.* 9. *for* 1st. *r.* 17th. p. 144. *l.* 1. *for* that *r.* tho', p. 165. *l.* 15. *r.* Precedent, p. 173. *l.* 21. *r.* Marchers, p. 174. *l. ult. dele* we, p. 184. *l.* 24. *r.* consider only, p. 195. *l.* 19. *r.* express, p. 200. *l.* 4. *r.* Poyning's, p. 201. *l.* 21. *and* 22. *r.* 1. As &c. p. 202. *l. ult. r.* who, with his States, p. 204. *l.* 23. *for* did *r.* does, p. 212. *l.* 9. *for* there *r.* here.

www.ingramcontent.com/pod-product-compliance
Lightning Source LLC
Chambersburg PA
CBHW021837230426
43669CB00008B/997